AF487924

Twin Flame Love

Soulmate Poetry

by

N.R.Hart

Monday Creek Publishing
Ohio USA

Titles by N.R.Hart

Poetry and Pearls
Poetry and Pearls II
Love Poems to No One
Beauty and Her Beast
The Last of the Romantics
Twin Flame Love: Soulmate Poetry

“We do not choose who we love but rather, our souls choose for us.” ©
– N.R.Hart

“Living for the day our worlds finally collide.” ©
– N.R.Hart

"When love exists on a soul level it
becomes something else entirely...
unfathomable , unbreakable,
undeniable. Eternal." ©
- N.R.Hart

Table of Contents

"Legend has it there is always a reason why souls meet." – N.R.Hart, *Beauty and the Beast*

Introduction

The Soulmate and Twin Flame theory can be traced all the way back to ancient history with Greek Mythology and Chinese Folklore.

According to Greek Mythology, humans were originally created with four arms, four legs and a head with two faces. The ancient god Zeus split them into two separate parts condemning them to spend the rest of their lives searching for their other halves. According to the myth of Chinese Legend, the two people connected by the Red String of Fate are destined lovers, regardless of time, place, or circumstance.

One must first understand the difference between a soulmate and a twin flame. A soulmate can be a friend, a romantic partner, a family member, or something else in your life. A soulmate is a person with whom you have an immediate connection with. Soulmates are naturally compatible and bring out the best in each other. You share a strong bond with them and have many common interests. You can have more than one soulmate in your lifetime.

A twin flame is your twin soul and divine counterpart. A friend or lover, but typically both. It is a once-in-a-lifetime bond and you share an intense connection. Sometimes, the connection is so strong, it can bring out both your positive and negative sides, revealing your strengths and weaknesses. Whatever you see in your twin lies within you, transforming you into your higher purpose in life. Since your souls have ascended to a higher level, you share a divine love.

There is only one twin flame in your lifetime and not everyone has recognized theirs. You can live your whole life without meeting them. However, if you are fortunate to have found your twin flame, make no mistake, you will know in the deepest crevice of your soul it is them. This marks a *before* and *after* in your life.

Whether you believe in soulmates or twin flames or both, the Universe works in strange and mysterious ways. There are no accidental meetings between souls, they are meant to cross paths for a reason. We don't always understand it as it is happening, or we can't put a name to it at the time, but the reasons become apparent later in our lives.

You will find new and old soulmate/twin flame poems in this collection. Maybe I have been writing this story all along. Maybe this journey is your journey. If you somehow see yourself in my words, find yourself in my words, feel yourself in my words, then maybe my story... is your story.

"Our souls fell in love long before we ever knew." – N.R.Hart, *Poetry and Pearls*

A Winter Season

"An ache only you can fill." ©

N.R.Hart

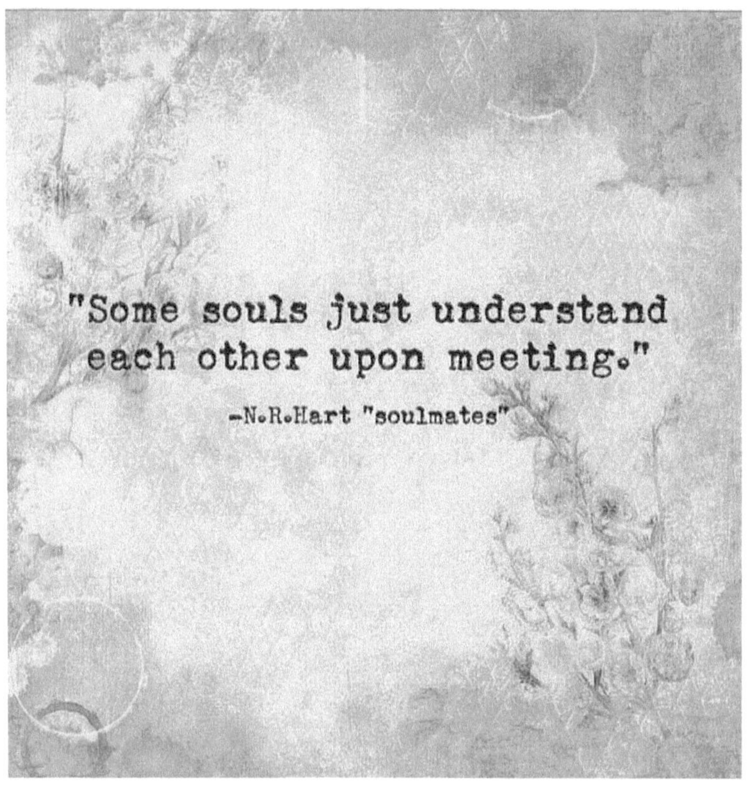
"Some souls just understand
each other upon meeting."

-N.R.Hart "soulmates"

Some may not believe
in the soulmate twin flame
theory
but whatever you believe
understand this
the universe holds mysteries
we know nothing of...
because some souls have an
unexplainable
connection to each other
because some souls are destined
to find one another
because some souls seem
too familiar to each other
because some souls just
understand
each other upon meeting.
N.R.Hart"soultheory"

"Maybe she needed someone
to show her how to live
and he needed someone
to show him how to love.

-N.R.Hart   "Beauty and the Beast

"Twin Flame"

You will know
the moment
you come upon your
Twin Flame.
They will start
a fire in you
that will not die.

-N.R.Hart ©2018

Maybe we are made up
of almosts.
The almost fairytale.
The almost romance.
The almost love of my life.
The almost happy ending.
Because, we were almost perfect.
Maybe I would rather have the almost
with you than the everything
with anyone else.
                    -N.R.Hart , Almost

Queen

You don't know this new me
I am not the naive one
anymore
I turned my pain into the most
beautiful poetry
I took all my brilliant pieces
and built myself an Empire.

-N.R.Hart

Restless nights
thoughts of you
quietly stir,
even in silence
in the stillness
of every night
I can still feel
your soul
touching mine.

-N.R.Hart

Betrayal

I gave you more than
I gave myself
only to realize
how little it mattered
how little "i" mattered
to you in the end
so loyal to you
that the only thing worse
than your betrayal
was that of my own heart.

N.R.Hart , "betrayal"

Distance tried to come
between them
so did life...
but they were always
connected
sometimes with words
sometimes with silence
sometimes with souls
nothing could stop it
not even time itself.

-N.R.Hart, connected

I liked it best when
he took control
how he possessed me
completely
the way I belonged to him
and he to me
and this kind of power makes
you beautifully vulnerable
in ways that you show
your true self.
He was my safe place...
I loved him because
I could be me in every way
others never see.
-N.R.Hart

If I keep writing
about you...
will I keep falling in love
all over again?

N.R.Hart

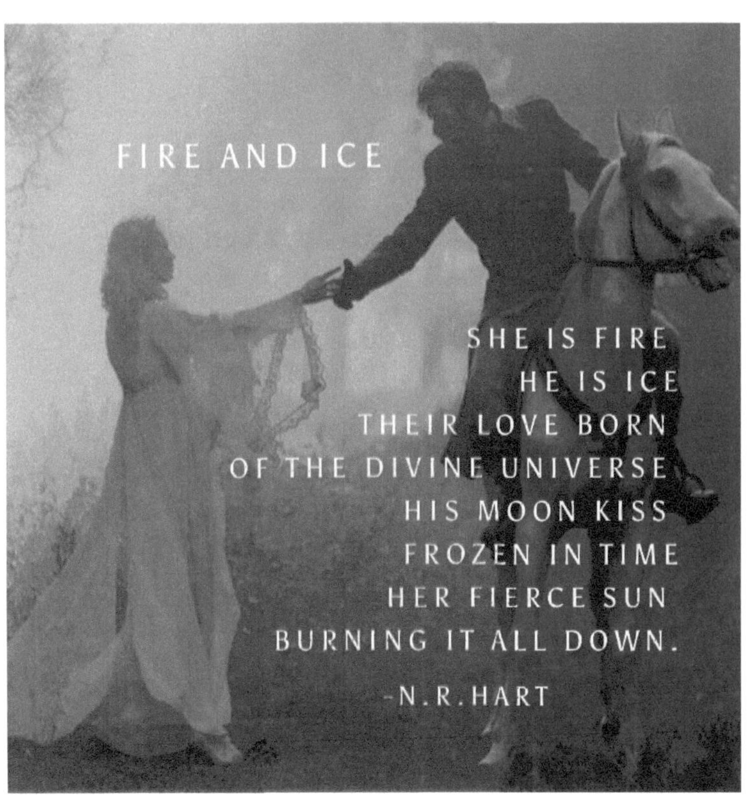
FIRE AND ICE

SHE IS FIRE
HE IS ICE
THEIR LOVE BORN
OF THE DIVINE UNIVERSE
HIS MOON KISS
FROZEN IN TIME
HER FIERCE SUN
BURNING IT ALL DOWN.

-N.R.HART

A Cautionary Tale

There was once a boy
and there was once a girl
and they loved each other
from long ago.
Did she love too much
and him not enough
Where did the time go...
Do they love one another,
still?
Does true love really
conquer all?
This...we will never know.

-N.R.Hart

Heart ache

And, when she was gone
he was never the same
after that.
His heart ached.
He carried a deep sadness
in his eyes.
She took a part of him with her.
A part of himself he missed.
There was an inner spirituality
which connected her with him.
He never again , felt whole.
He is still searching for his
soul...
when it was her, all along.

        -N.R.Hart

Twin Flames

It was as if they were connected on a
different plane from everything else;
and it was the two of them in their own
little world.
How they had a secret language between souls
and their fiery energy fed off each other.
They didn't always need words because
they could communicate through silence.
They had each other memorized and they
could feel one another through time
and space.
Their souls were always touching
like twin flames, existing within each other
and burning through everything else.

They were only certain of one thing.
It felt right to be with one another.

—N.R.Hart *"twin flames"*

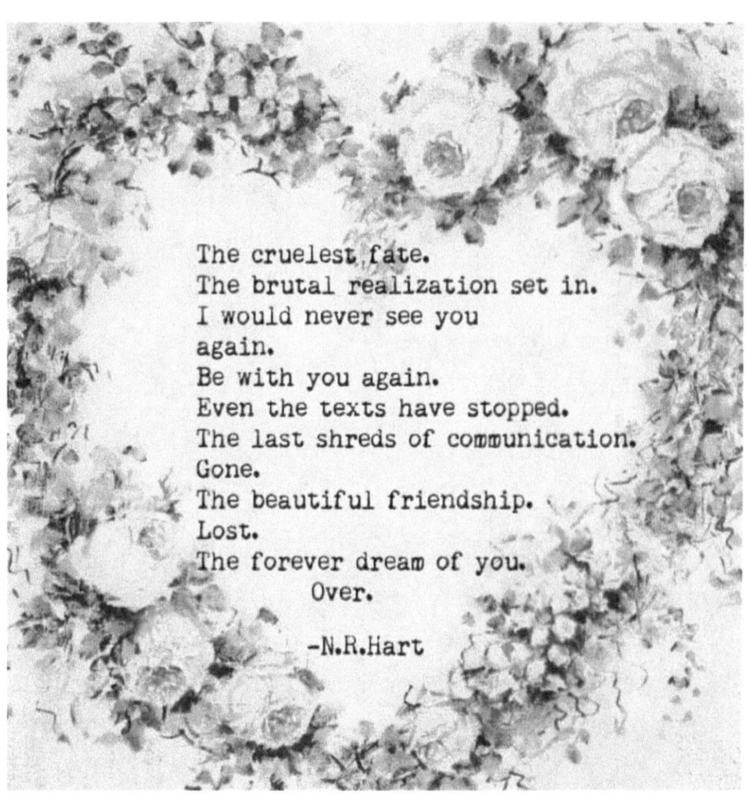
The cruelest fate.
The brutal realization set in.
I would never see you
again.
Be with you again.
Even the texts have stopped.
The last shreds of communication.
Gone.
The beautiful friendship.
Lost.
The forever dream of you.
          Over.

     -N.R.Hart

I loved you with my eyes
because they only saw
the good in you.
I loved you with my mind
because I never ran
out of words for you.
I loved you with my heart
because it still beats your
name.
But mostly, I loved you with
my soul.
Because my soul always
remembers.
Because my soul never forgets.

-N.R.Hart, I Loved You With My Soul

"Irreplaceable"

And, I think you will always
be the one who knows me best,
and I will always be the one
who knows you best.
When you finally find someone
who gets you, really gets you...
for the first time in your life
you feel "seen".
The way we watch for each other.
The way we wait for each other.
Not everything in life is
replaceable.
Some people happen only once.
Because, I still look for you...
Because, you were the only one
who has ever been able to find
me...
                    -N.R.Hart

She was an unexpected
love in his life
she never gave up
on him...
he never had that
before with anyone
and...he loved that
about her.
-N.R.Hart

TWIN FLAME

Do you remember that day
we drove until dusk
I kissed you in every
beautiful place
leaving our trace.
I kissed you in your car
my lips on your neck
still carries my scent.
I kissed you under the moon
my soul and your soul
together as one.
I kissed you under the sun
passions ignite
twin flames for life.
Half our lives.
A lifetime of love...
Somehow, wiped out.
Somehow, long gone.

    -N.R.Hart Twin Flame

You see, I kept losing
versions of you
and I didn't want to lose
any more of you.
This watered-down version
of you
this indifference
this not quite friends
not quite anything, really.
I wanted to keep the version
of you I loved best.
The one that loved me.

-N.R.Hart, The one that loved me

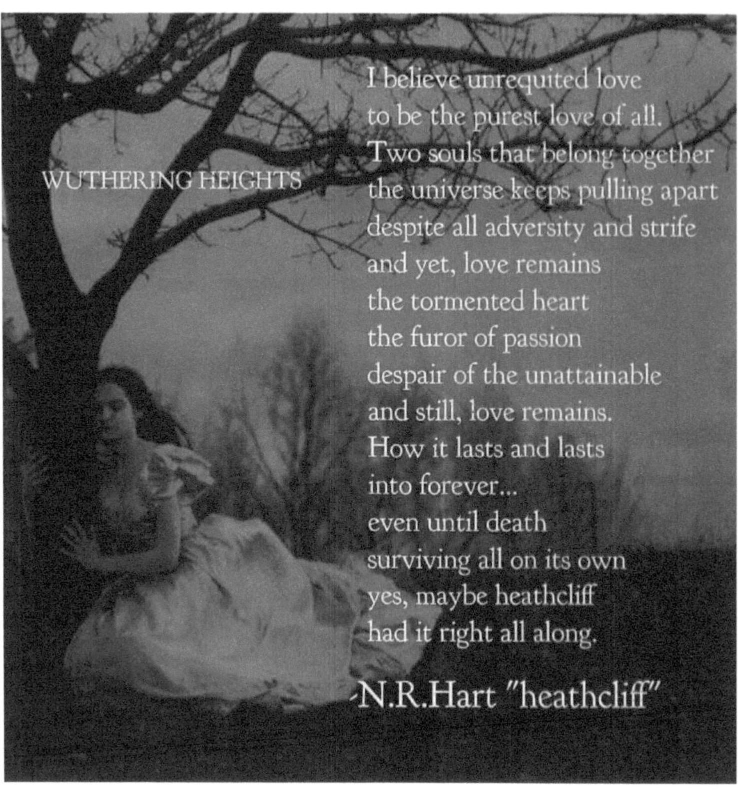

WUTHERING HEIGHTS

I believe unrequited love
to be the purest love of all.
Two souls that belong together
the universe keeps pulling apart
despite all adversity and strife
and yet, love remains
the tormented heart
the furor of passion
despair of the unattainable
and still, love remains.
How it lasts and lasts
into forever...
even until death
surviving all on its own
yes, maybe heathcliff
had it right all along.

N.R.Hart "heathcliff"

I can't tell you
the exact moment
I fell in love with you
but, maybe it was the way
your eyes looked different
that day
they seemed a little
deeper and your smile
a little sweeter
how your touch lingered
on me
a little longer
because, everything felt
different that day...
and I knew I would never
be the same again.

-N.R.Hart "the day I fell in love"

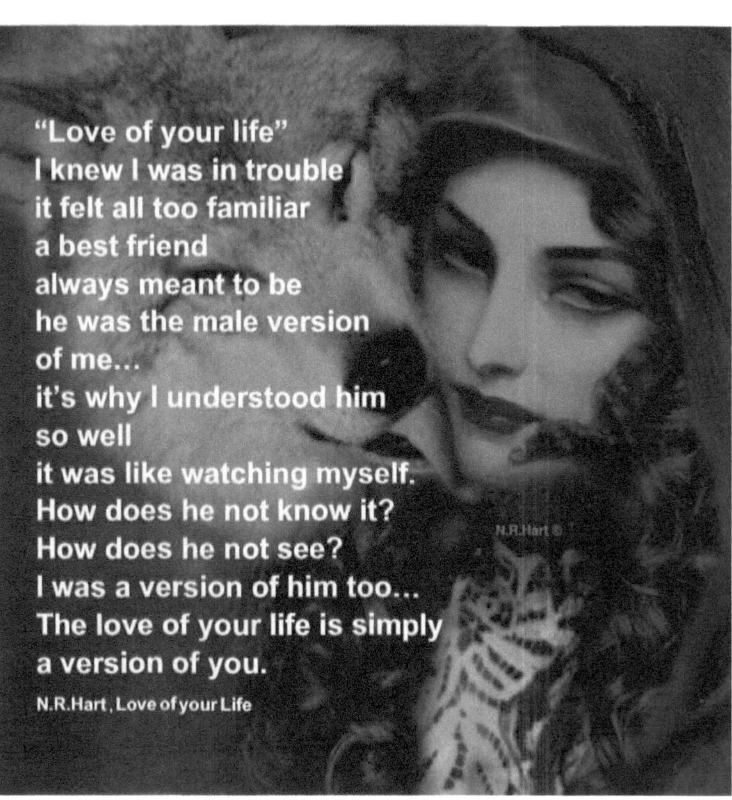

"Love of your life"
I knew I was in trouble
it felt all too familiar
a best friend
always meant to be
he was the male version
of me...
it's why I understood him
so well
it was like watching myself.
How does he not know it?
How does he not see?
I was a version of him too...
The love of your life is simply
a version of you.

N.R.Hart, Love of your Life

Sometimes...
our own love story
is right in front
of us
and we are too blind
to see it.
And, sometimes we find
our soulmate in a best
friend.
And, sometimes it has
been right there... all
along.

—N.R.Hart "Love Story"

"it should have been you"

I wanted to share so many
things with you
I wanted you to be a part of
so many things in my life
that should have been yours
too.
I wanted you to be there
for all of it
but you won't be there
for any of it
how someone will take
your place...
when it should have been
you.

-N.R.Hart "missing things"

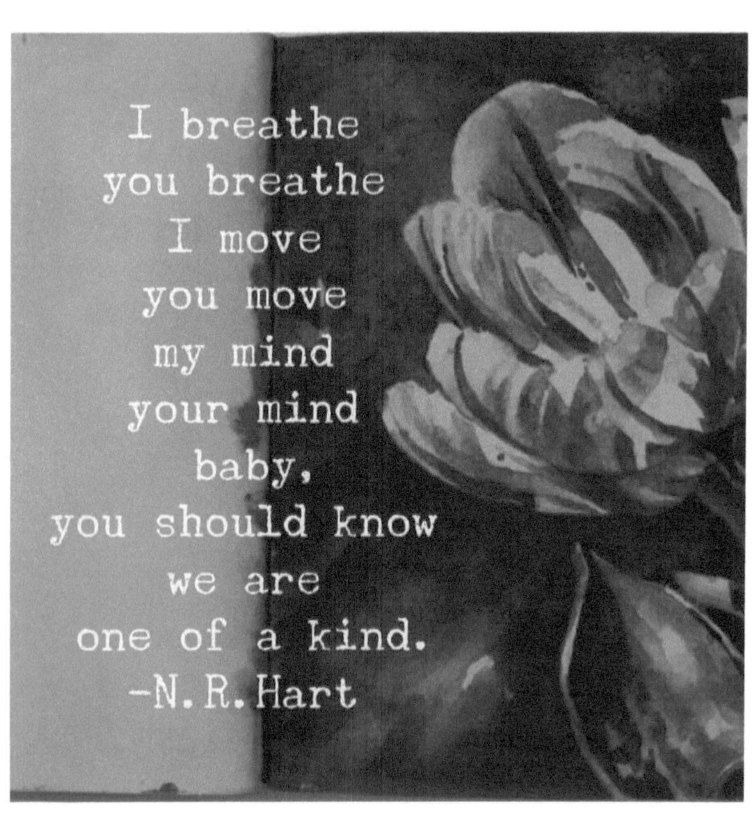

I breathe
you breathe
I move
you move
my mind
your mind
baby,
you should know
we are
one of a kind.
-N.R.Hart

Reflection

We were destined to meet
no matter the distance
we return to each other
again and again.
It's that once in a lifetime
connection, the one that
makes you feel more alive
just sitting next to them;
even the silence is comfortable
because you feel more complete
in their presence.
I don't know what it is about
you ... only that
when I look into your eyes
I see a reflection of my soul
staring back at me. -N.R.Hart

He said to her
don't fall in love
with me...
she thought
to herself
silly boy, we are best
friends...
we've been madly in love
since the day we met.
-N.R.Hart "Poetry and Pearls"

You want what you can't
have so you try settling
once more.
But, don't you know?
The things that come easy
won't last
and the things that last long
won't come easy.
And, that's how you know
the difference.
And, that's how you know
when it's love.

-N.R.Hart "that's how you know"

We were soul deep
in love
our souls loved
one another
long before we ever knew
this was a once
in a lifetime love.
One we cannot undo.
-N.R.Hart

"Soulmates"

Soulmates aren't just anyone you meet.
They are souls you instantly have a connection
with.
They are souls who sometimes
know you better than you know
yourself.
They are the ones who can almost hear your
thoughts without you uttering a word.
You find comfort in their presence and you are
understood in their silence.
They represent love and danger and you come
alive with them near.
You have a longing to know them...
an ache only they can fill.

-N.R.Hart "Soulmates"

And, there is a reason why
you can't walk away
there is a reason why you
stay.
It is because we belonged
to each other from the start.
You don't know this but
we secretly rescue each other...
from life, from love, from
everything.
Your soul and my soul are
the same.
We exist in each other.
And, the only thing scarier
than staying is leaving because
our souls already knew we
could never part. -N.R.Hart
"Souls"

All those days
I wasn't the same
maybe
it was the most me
I'd ever be
all those feelings
I lived and
dwelt
loving you...
was the most
I had ever felt.

-N.R.Hart , the most me

The Saddest Thing (part II)

You could see the way they looked
at each other
like nothing else existed in the
world except the two of them.
They were all of it.
Best friends, lovers, soulmates.
But, there are no more looks.
No more playful words of affection
between them.
No more teasing. No more quarreling.
No more making up. No more love.
Just silence.
And, now ... the silence only teaches
them how to live without you.
When two people with so much love
for each other are learning to live
without each other ... well, that is
the saddest existence of all.

-N.R.Hart

Favorite Feeling

You were always
my favorite feeling
my favorite place...
where I could be me
and you could be you
and we could just be...
it's why we kept
coming back
the place we felt free.

-N.R.Hart

Twin Flame - "Your greatest soul connection"
Your twin flame will trigger your deepest feelings,
emotions and passions.
Twin Flames may flee the connection because
their presence is such an overwhelming love
in their lives, only to try and replace it with
someone else.
But, what you will come to find is, after the novelty
of a new connection wears off,
the twinflame connection can never be replaced
with anyone else.
You will have only one Twin Flame in your lifetime
and they will search their entire lives in those
around them for what is missing and they will
never find it.
Because your twin flame is your perfect match.
They will touch your soul on a cosmic level
unlike anyone else can or will.
They are your greatest soul connection. -N.R.Hart

Twin Flames "A Romantic Tragedy" 

You meet your twin flame in the most unexpected manner
and you instantly become mesmerized by them. You feel things
for them you never felt before with anyone. You fall in love with
their soul.

You are not searching for them yet, they appear as divine timing
sent by the Universe. You are magnetically drawn to them and they
energize you physically making you feel alive.

You are spiritually-aligned and your twin flame meets you at a level
of self-awakening where you are forced to confront your own soul.
They are the one soul that leads you back to your true authentic-self.
You are eternally connected and it is the one love that never fades
and only gets stronger with time.

Do twin flames always end up together?

They share a mental telepathy so strong, they can't help but feel
each other, their souls are always touching.

*The Universe deals the cruelest fate, bringing twin souls together,
while the world keeps coming between them. You see, they just can't stay away
from one another. The simple truth is, together or apart, they will always
belong to each other. They will always suffer for each other.*

They asked her, I thought Twin Flames is a Love Story?
And she answered back, aren't all the best stories ... Tragedies?
-N.R.Hart

Because no one
makes me
happier sadder
crazier
devastatingly
hopelessly
tragically in love ...
more than you.

-N.R.Hart

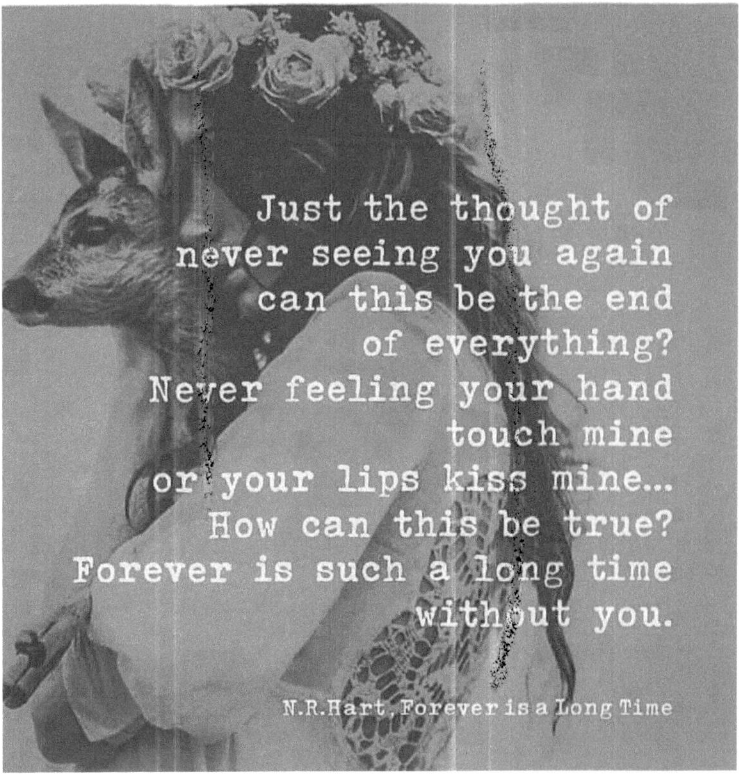

Just the thought of
never seeing you again
can this be the end
of everything?
Never feeling your hand
touch mine
or your lips kiss mine...
How can this be true?
Forever is such a long time
without you.

N.R.Hart, Forever is a Long Time

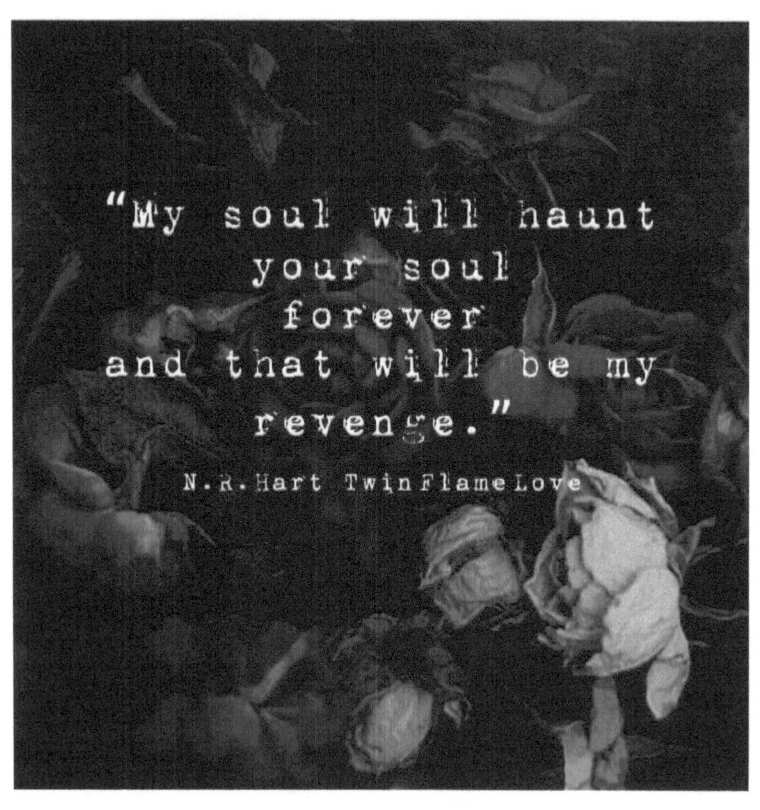

"My soul will haunt
your soul
forever
and that will be my
revenge."
N.R.Hart TwinFlameLove

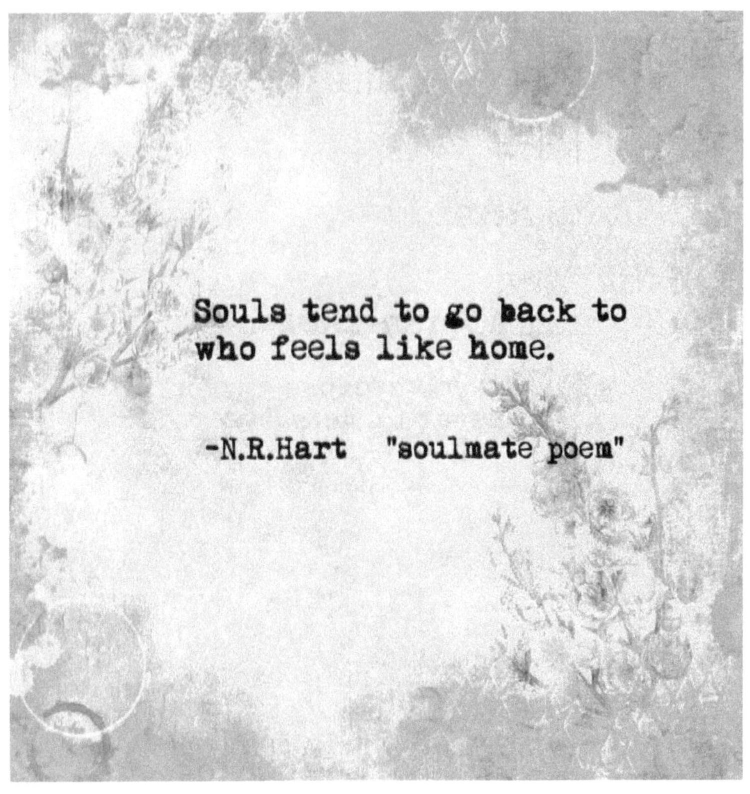
Souls tend to go back to
who feels like home.

-N.R.Hart   "soulmate poem"

A Spring Season

"I love you because my soul
never forgets." ©

N.R.Hart

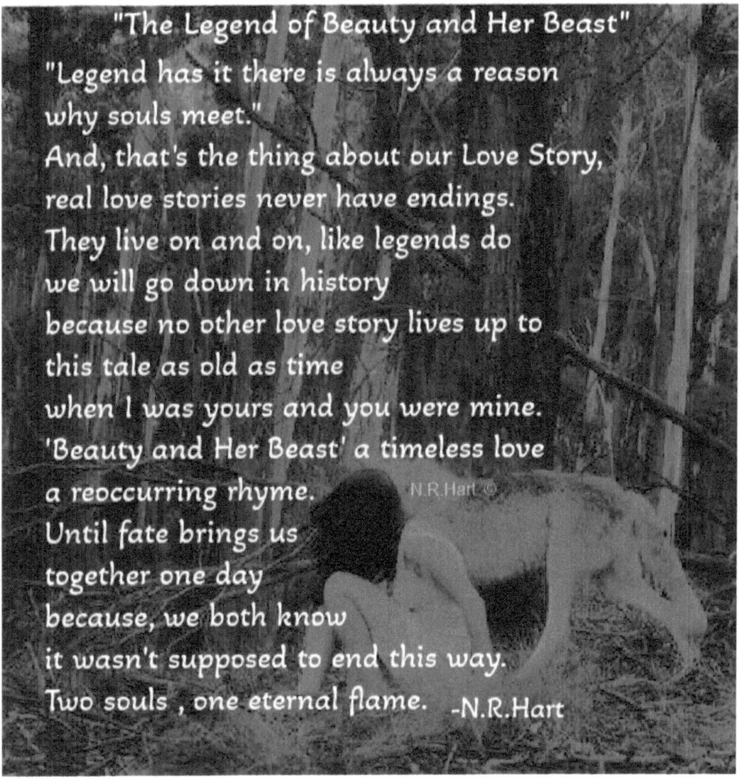

"The Legend of Beauty and Her Beast"
"Legend has it there is always a reason
why souls meet."
And, that's the thing about our Love Story,
real love stories never have endings.
They live on and on, like legends do
we will go down in history
because no other love story lives up to
this tale as old as time
when I was yours and you were mine.
'Beauty and Her Beast' a timeless love
a reoccurring rhyme.
Until fate brings us
together one day
because, we both know
it wasn't supposed to end this way.
Two souls , one eternal flame.   -N.R.Hart

I waited and waited
but you never did show
I always thought you somehow
loved me...
how was it I didn't know?
-N.R.Hart "Poetry and Pearls"

Otherworldly 

They had a deep connection
a burning chemistry
they fit together
like they had always
known each other.
When she was around him
she felt more like herself.
There was a feeling
that this was bigger
than both of them.
She didn't understand it
but she knew it changed her
forever.
It was a different world now.

-N.R.Hart

Some moments
are inevitable
they must happen.
Like a kiss....
nothing can stop it.
Destiny had already
been decided.   —N. R. Hart

She felt something was different
about him the moment she laid eyes on him
and she thought to herself
he will be a dangerous one...
not only because their souls were
magically drawn to each other
beyond all reason but this powerful force
towards one another overtook her...
a complete surrendering of souls
and it scared her what she might do for him.
It was a chaotic love...a sweet creeping
madness between them like nothing she had
ever experienced before. And once you have
experienced euphoric passion...
there was no going back to ordinary love.
Maybe...just maybe...a consuming love
like that cannot last and her cruelest fate
she had a taste of something she couldn't
live without...yet was destined to.

N.R. Hart || a love like that

Captivated

There is no other soul for her.
He challenges her. He scares her.
He surprises her. He captivates her.
He is either the best thing for her
or the worst thing or maybe both...
right or wrong none of that matters
because...
she is going to love him anyway.

-N.R.Hart

They never knew
they were addicted to
each other
until they tried to stop.

N.R.Hart

down in flames

You were my best friend
i had a crush on
you meant everything
so i kissed you
and,
my soul cracked open
my whole world
went down in flames.

-N.R.Hart

First Kiss

There has always been
something unspoken
between us
from the day
we first met...
and years later
our first kiss
and how you knew
before I did
that we always wanted
each other...
from that moment on
we couldn't stay away
it was always there...
something rare
something silent
something wild.
N.R.Hart Something Unspoken

Heart & Soul

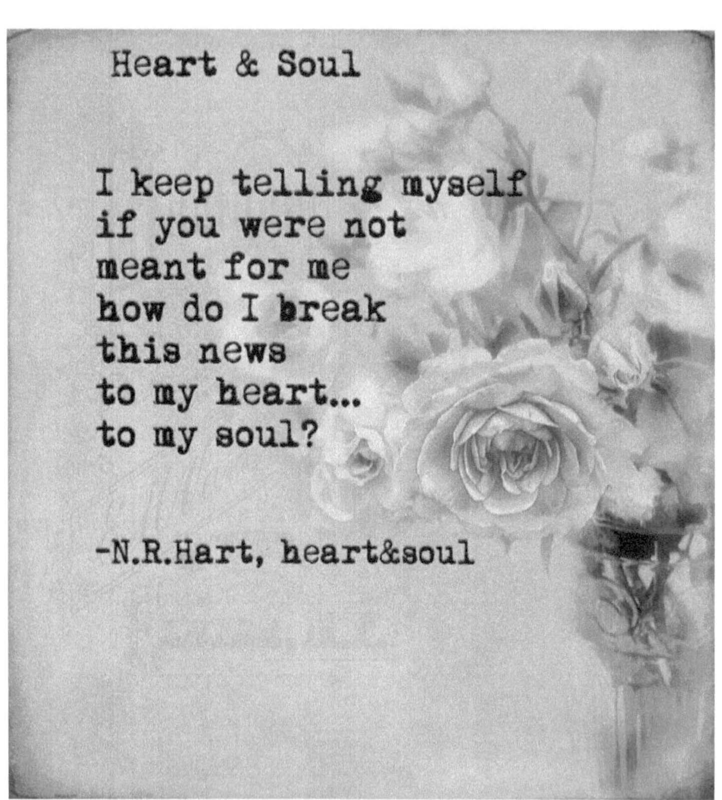
I keep telling myself
if you were not
meant for me
how do I break
this news
to my heart...
to my soul?

-N.R.Hart, heart&soul

It happens once in a lifetime
a divine meeting between souls
fated and predestined
by the universe
an encounter so right it feels like
home.
It's your soul falling in love
with another soul.
Pay attention it happens only once
and never again.

-N.R.Hart "twinflame"

HEARTSTRINGS

SHE NEVER WANTED PROMISES
SHE ONLY WANTED YOU.
IT'S WHY SHE KEPT REACHING
FOR YOU. A SMALL TUG ON
YOUR HEARTSTRINGS.
 AND ALL SHE EVER REALLY
NEEDED WAS FOR YOU TO
TUG BACK TO KEEP HER THERE.

-N.R.HART

Heaven and Hell

I am convinced there is one love
in your lifetime that you can never
forget and you will never get over.
It is different from all the rest
because it marks a before and after
them...in your life.
And it is the most terrifying kind
of love because you experience
a passion that is out of control...
it excites you and scares you
at the same time. You become addicted
to that feeling of being alive.
And this kind of love...and only
this kind you would move heaven
and earth...meet them on the other
side of hell...just to feel it again.

N.R.Hart

MY SOUL IS A HOPELESS
ROMANTIC
AND HOW IT KEEPS RUNNING
AND RUNNING TO YOU.
N.R.Hart ©

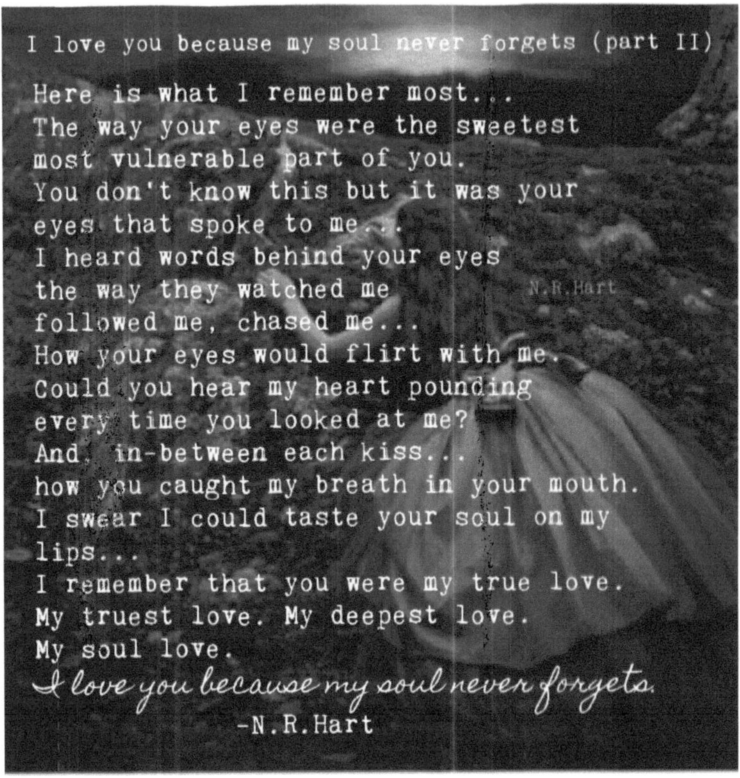

I love you because my soul never forgets (part II)

Here is what I remember most...
The way your eyes were the sweetest
most vulnerable part of you.
You don't know this but it was your
eyes that spoke to me...
I heard words behind your eyes
the way they watched me
followed me, chased me...
How your eyes would flirt with me.
Could you hear my heart pounding
every time you looked at me?
And, in-between each kiss...
how you caught my breath in your mouth.
I swear I could taste your soul on my
lips...
I remember that you were my true love.
My truest love. My deepest love.
My soul love.
I love you because my soul never forgets.
                    -N.R.Hart

She was dreaming the same dream
again ...
that he would come for her
like he always did
because nothing is the same
with him gone
all she wanted was to climb
onto his lap
curling up next to him
and breathe in his familiar
scent
telling him how much she missed
the way they were
when they're together
because nothing could ever replace
the way they were
and ... they both knew it.

-N.R.Hart, Dream (the way they were)

Just friends

We were always a little
more than friends
even when we were
just friends.
It was always more
than that.
We were everything.
It's why we are strangers
now
it's why everything...
turned to nothing.

N.R.Hart , Twin Flames

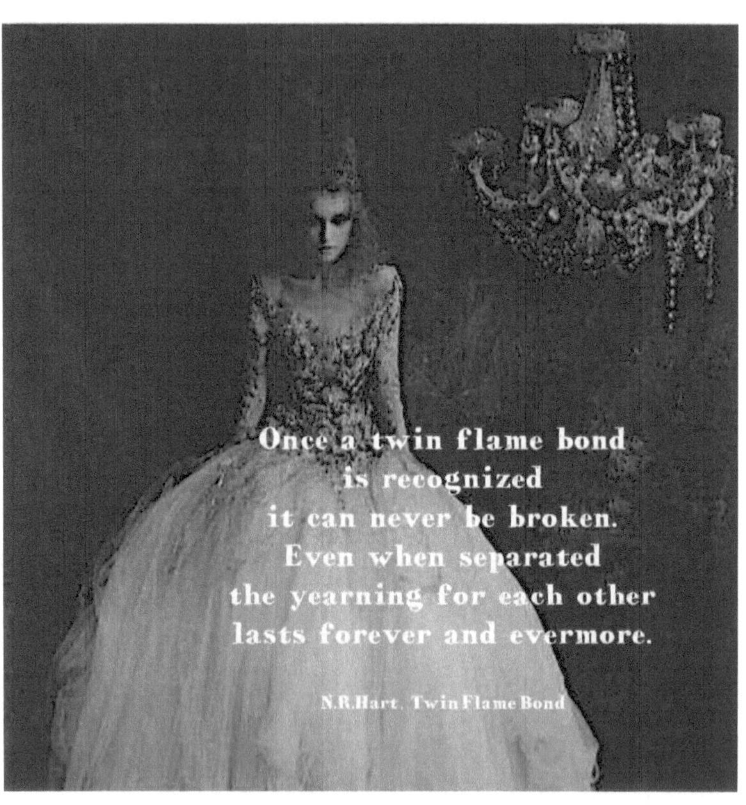

Once a twin flame bond
is recognized
it can never be broken.
Even when separated
the yearning for each other
lasts forever and evermore.

N.R.Hart, Twin Flame Bond

I was drawn to you in ways
I did not understand like
a moth to a flame
you invoke a sense of exhilaration
making me feel alive...
the very thought of you makes
my blood boil orange
my heart thundering inside my chest
butterflies crashing into my ribs
you can seduce with just one word
as I shiver in anticipation
dying for your touch.
You are all things forbidden
and everything I crave...
I am addicted to the way you make
me feel...
and, you are everything I should
not want yet, I would do it all over
again. -N.R. Hart "forbidden"

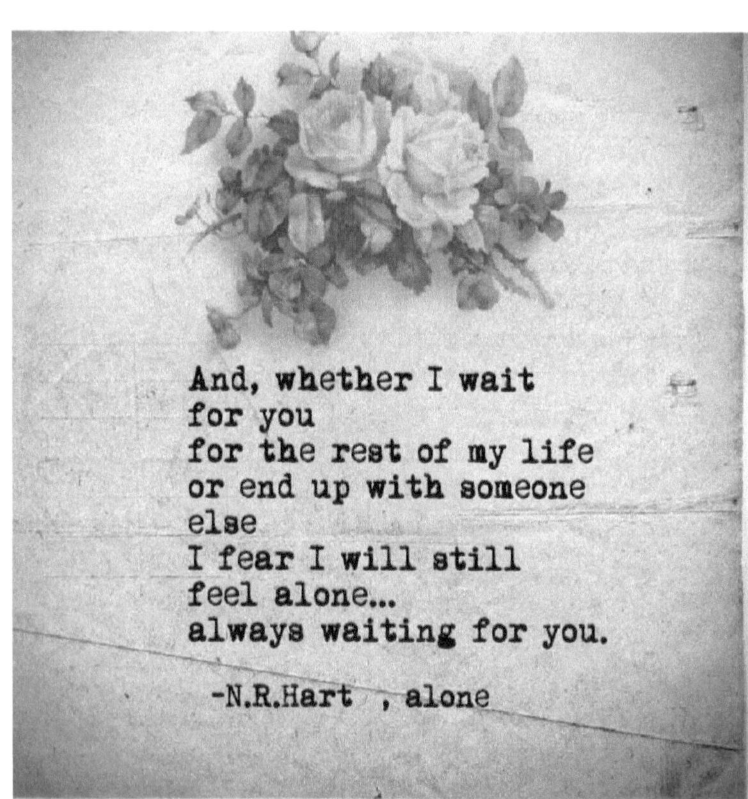

And, whether I wait
for you
for the rest of my life
or end up with someone
else
I fear I will still
feel alone...
always waiting for you.

-N.R.Hart , alone

Quiet Magnificence

I once told you I would never give up on you.
All it takes is one person to believe in you.
Just one. And, you will start believing in
yourself too.
Some souls just know to believe in one another.
It feels as though their soul is living inside you.
And giving up on them would mean giving up
on yourself too. Let me be the one who doesn't
give up on you. That believes in you.
I want to be the one.
To love you is to love me.
And, while the others don't notice your quiet
magnificence. I do. I always do.

-N.R.Hart

"Memorized"

You and I,
the best of friends
we laugh and play
but, for another day
mostly silence is our way.
You and I,
lovers words run dry
or maybe we just don't try
Because, you and I
we are just we,
we have each other
memorized
and that has always been
enough for me.
                    -N.R.Hart

Her eyes
made love
to his soul
long
before her
body touched
his.
-N.R.Hart

And, deep down you know
that no one will understand you
in the way that I do
no one will get you in the way
that I get you.
I challenged you to be yourself.
And, this is why you will always
settle for less than you need.
And, this is why you will always
want more. N.R.Hart. "more"

You will always be that one.
That one for me.
The one I run to day or night
you are my only escape route.
The one I want to spend countless
hours with...doing nothing.
My midnight text, my 3 a.m. lust
my daydream at dawn.
The one I won't bother asking where
you have been because it never even
mattered.
You are my sweetest sin, my weakest
link...my kryptonite.
The one I always want.
And, you are the one where I tell
myself to stop this madness because
after all, enough is enough.
But, it never is. Never. -N.R.Hart

                              "my kryptonite"

"Once more"

oh, how I tried to breathe life back
into these sacred ashes of this tragic
romance...
I refuse to go quietly
not without claw marks and desperate
kisses
and trembling words and embers still
smouldering.
I clung to the warmest flame
of our love with poems lit and caught
fire
leaving me here where you found me
to burn at your mercy , once more ...
waiting for you to be brave enough
to love me.

-N.R.Hart

"Simple and Complicated"

When they asked her
what was it about him
that made her feel
this way...
she could never really explain
what he did to her
she felt things with him
she never felt before
with anyone.
She only knew that when she
was with him
she was the happiest she had
ever been.
It was as simple and as
complicated as that.
-N.R.Hart

"Twin Flame"

It's that rare
connection
the one that's
unexplainable
a chemistry that
is undeniable
a love unlike any
other.

-N.R.Hart , Twin Flame Love

Twin Flame

You finally met
your match
the one who challenged you
to be yourself
and that scared you
more than anything
you couldn't handle the flame
you were afraid to burn
you ran from the fire
you ran from me
you ran from us
you ran from yourself. -N.R.Hart

                "Sacred Pact"
It's not that I am living
in the past...
it's just that I don't want
to be anywhere else
I've seen the future
without you...
and something is missing
you are what's missing...
I know when something looks
different, feels different,
is different...from the rest
when the love is rare
the flame is pure
the connection is true
this sacred pact, with you.
They say you can't live in the past,
and I say, you can try and live
in the present all you want,
but you look back.
You keep looking back...

-N.R.Hart, Twin Flame Love

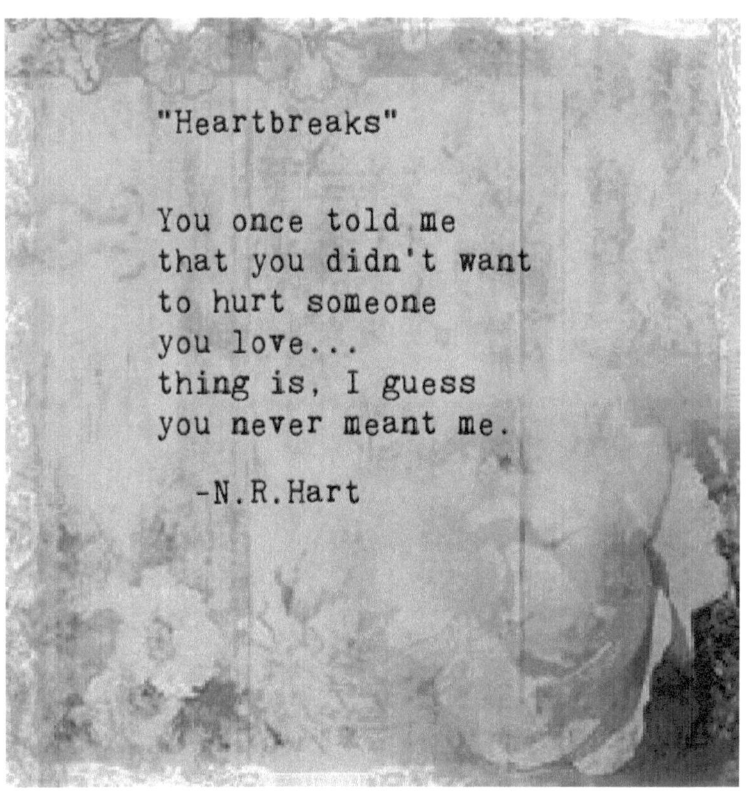
"Heartbreaks"

You once told me
that you didn't want
to hurt someone
you love...
thing is, I guess
you never meant me.

-N.R.Hart

She feels him in a way
she has never felt
anyone before
and this is how her soul knows
he is hers.
-N.R.Hart   soul love

Soulmate poem

During your lifetime there
will be one person who is
unlike any other. You will
know this because you feel
different around them. You feel
more like yourself because you
can sense them deep in your soul.
You come alive with them near.
You can tell them anything
and their love for you
is unconditional.
This person is your best friend
and your soulmate.
You will not find anyone like
them again. Never let them go.

-N.R.Hart, Soulmate Poem

Written in the Stars

There was always something
inevitable about us. How we
watched our friendship bloom
into so much more ...
We were the lovers who kept finding
one another again and again
no matter how many times the world came
between us.
Because when the Universe gives you more
than you bargained for,
you accept your fate.
A love so out of this world, you won't
know what to do with it all.
A journey you can't walk away from.
You will love it. You will hate it.
It will break you.
But, it will make you believe in bigger
things. Bigger than you.
It will make you believe in destiny.
In souls ...
It will make you believe in the stars.
                    -N.R.Hart

Meeting your twin flame will not
be a chance encounter but rather
your souls will recognize one another.
You will know it by how you feel
because you won't feel that way
with anyone but them.
Everything feels different, looks
different, is different.
The connection is so strong
and intense it may even scare
you....but you will not be able to
ignore it. You come alive around them
and the passion you experience
is out of control almost to the brink
of madness. And it is the most you
have ever felt.
You breathe differently now and every cell
inside you is on fire, and yet
they bring you a kind of peace you have
never known.
Your entire world is shaken..and yet
you are home. -N.R.Hart "twin flame"

Twin Flames part2

Twin flames also known as souls split
in two, literally the other half of your soul
is bound to another soul by familiarity and
forged by fire.
This pure energy of the cosmos connects these souls
on every level, mentally, spiritually, soulfully
and physically. They are continually drawn and
pulled towards one another in mysterious ways
through a powerful force of the universe
and return to each other again and again
like the crashing tides of the ocean.
Because this flame involves energy, elevating you
to a higher level of consciousness, the attraction
is so strong and fiery, it may even scare you off...
but, they will understand you in a way no one
ever has or will.
Once recognized as your twin flame , their presence
in your life will shake you up and at the same time,
make you feel at peace.
This "oneness" with another soul makes you feel whole
in ways you never have before. Like every dying star
in the universe has been brought back to life.
It feels like destiny to be with them. -N.R.Hart

I always knew we were different...
There is one true love story in your lifetime
that is unlike any other.
And, it will steal your soul for all eternity.
This kind of love feels different...
like nothing you have ever felt before or ever
will again. It was the most you have ever felt.
And, I never questioned how or why, because
loving you made me feel more like myself.
It went beyond all reason. It never made
sense. But, the greatest loves rarely do.
They just were and you lived them...
without trying to understand them.
It was a part of you. It was all of you. And,
it was different. And, we were different.
*"Because, even if I tried to explain us...they would
never understand."*   -N.R.Hart

"we were different..."

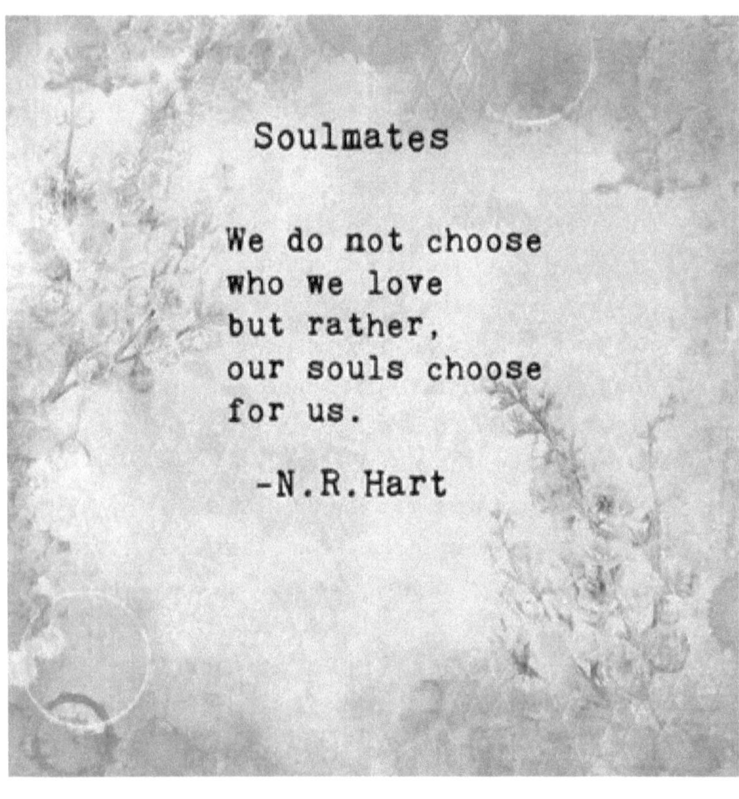

Soulmates

We do not choose
who we love
but rather,
our souls choose
for us.

-N.R.Hart

A Summer Season

"My soul breathes your name
my heart does the same." ©

N.R.Hart

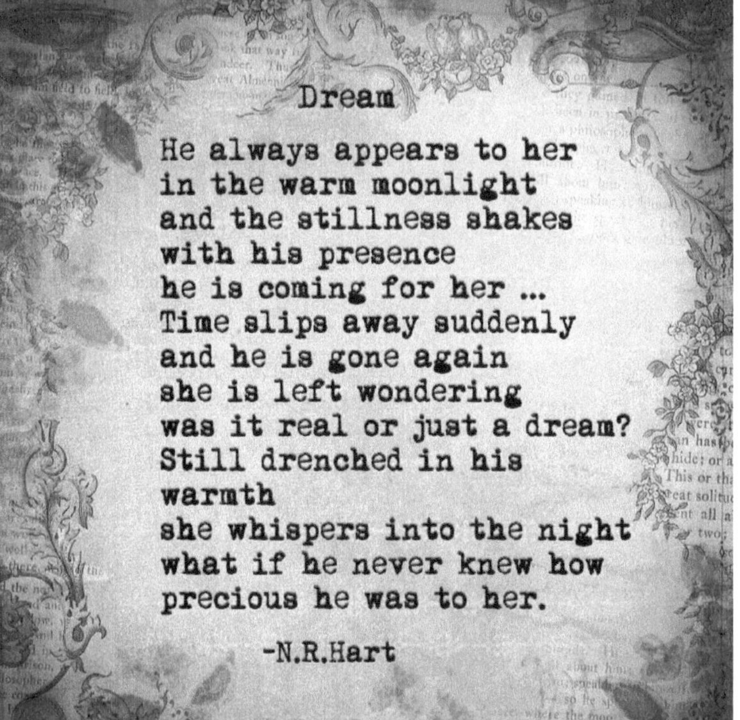

Dream

He always appears to her
in the warm moonlight
and the stillness shakes
with his presence
he is coming for her ...
Time slips away suddenly
and he is gone again
she is left wondering
was it real or just a dream?
Still drenched in his
warmth
she whispers into the night
what if he never knew how
precious he was to her.

-N.R.Hart

She said in a pleading whisper,
please don't go...
I will miss you so.
But, he left anyway
there will be someone like her again.
Until it finally hit him...
there will never be another her.
His heart...hurt.
His soul was in a constant state
of unrest.
He spent the rest of his life
searching for her.
But, he never found her.
Not ever again.

N.R.Hart "another her"

Beauty and her Beast

Most nights you lay there
next to her
while thinking of me
and you think no one knows
but I do....
because everyone knows
second best is never as good
as the original. -N.R.Hart

"The Original"

All I want
all I really want...
is to just keep talking
to you
and it doesn't matter what
we talk about
as long as you
are with me.
Just be with me...
And, we can figure out the rest
later.
- N.R.Hart

"Precious Things"

You stood there and watched her walk away
when all she wanted was to stay.
She had given you every chance
to make things right.
More chances than you ever deserved.
But...you didn't make it right, did you?
They say you don't know what you have
until it's gone.
But, she knew from the very beginning how
precious this love was. How deeply embedded
you were into her skin.
That's why she held on for as long as she
did. She so inherently understood about the
loss of a rare friendship.
The loss of a true love.
How much worse is it for her that she knew,
all along?
And, tried every way she could.
And, did you finally understand all at once,
that you never did enough?
Because, you don't know what you have
until it's gone.   -N.R.Hart

BEAUTY AND HER BEAST

It will happen one day
you know?
You will regret not fighting
for her
With her by your side
she will inspire you to achieve
your greatest work
your highest calling
as she does her own.
She will make you feel
as if anything is possible,
because with her, it is.
A once in a lifetime woman,
she will unleash the beast
inside the man.
You will regret not fighting for her
because she is worth the fight
because you will never feel whole
from betraying your soul.

N.R.HART, ONE DAY

A love like hers

And, he couldn't
forget about her
either...
because deep down
he knew he'd never
find another love
like hers.

-N.R.Hart

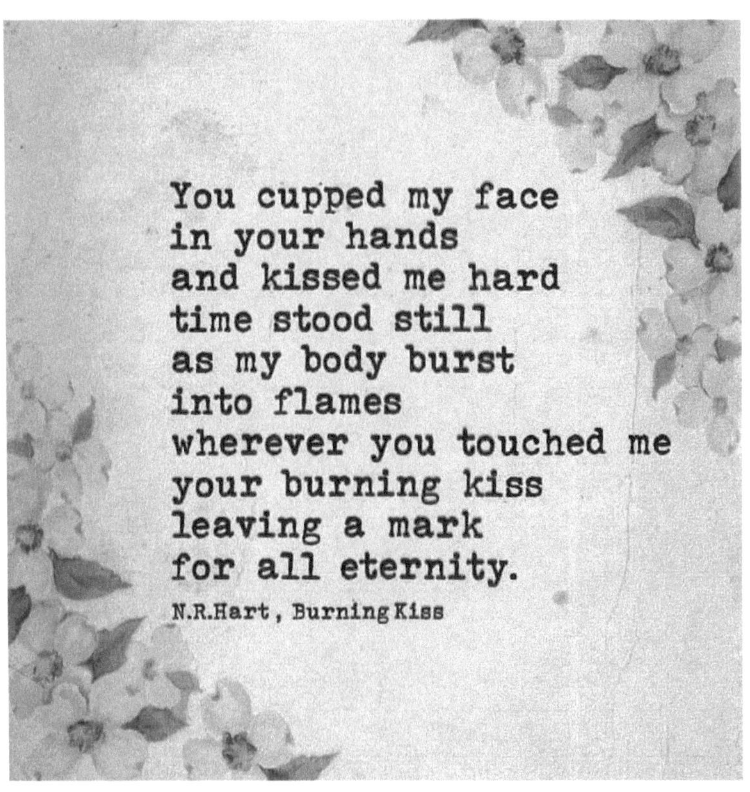

You cupped my face
in your hands
and kissed me hard
time stood still
as my body burst
into flames
wherever you touched me
your burning kiss
leaving a mark
for all eternity.

N.R.Hart, Burning Kiss

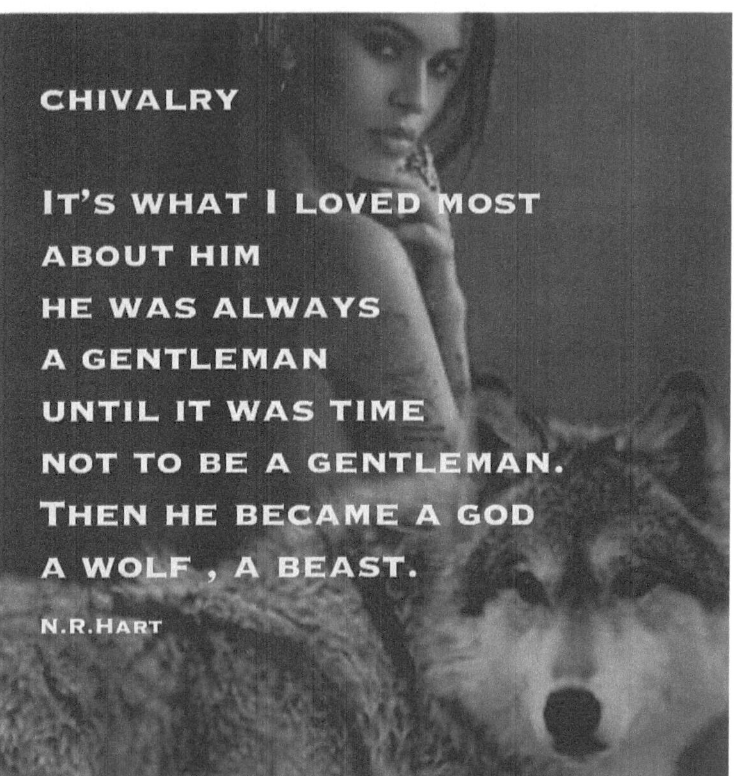
CHIVALRY

IT'S WHAT I LOVED MOST
ABOUT HIM
HE WAS ALWAYS
A GENTLEMAN
UNTIL IT WAS TIME
NOT TO BE A GENTLEMAN.
THEN HE BECAME A GOD
A WOLF , A BEAST.

N.R.HART

"Dangerous love"

I don't want to be the comfortable
one
I want to be the dangerous love.
The one you are mysteriously
drawn to
the one who keeps you up at night
makes your heart beat faster
an out of control love
that leaves you breathless.
I am not just any girl
I am your addiction.
The one you are wild for
the one you cannot live without.
I want to get under your skin and
stay there.
    -N.R.Hart

A deep hunger...
as our souls sank
into one another
and with one hard
thrust; he took me
all of me...
I wanted to be
taken.
I wanted to be his.

-N.R.Hart

My eyes my heart beg
for the crush of your strong
body as I sink my teeth
into your hot caving flesh
the smell of your dark musk
penetrating my lungs
your skin sticking hard
to mine
I plant treacherous pink kisses
wet deep kisses
sweet desperate smothering kisses
bite you taste you all of you
I will kiss you as if you are
my destiny
my love you will see
you can't forget me. - N.R. Hart

My love,
I look for you
everywhere
but,
I cannot find you
anywhere
and yet,
I feel you all the time.
N.R.Hart,   Feel you

She will be the girl
who loves you like no
other.
The girl whose kiss still
lingers
on your lips.
The girl whose memory
refuses to fade away.
She will be the girl
you won't ever
forget.
The one who got away.
She will be forever...
that girl.

—N.R.Hart "forever that girl"

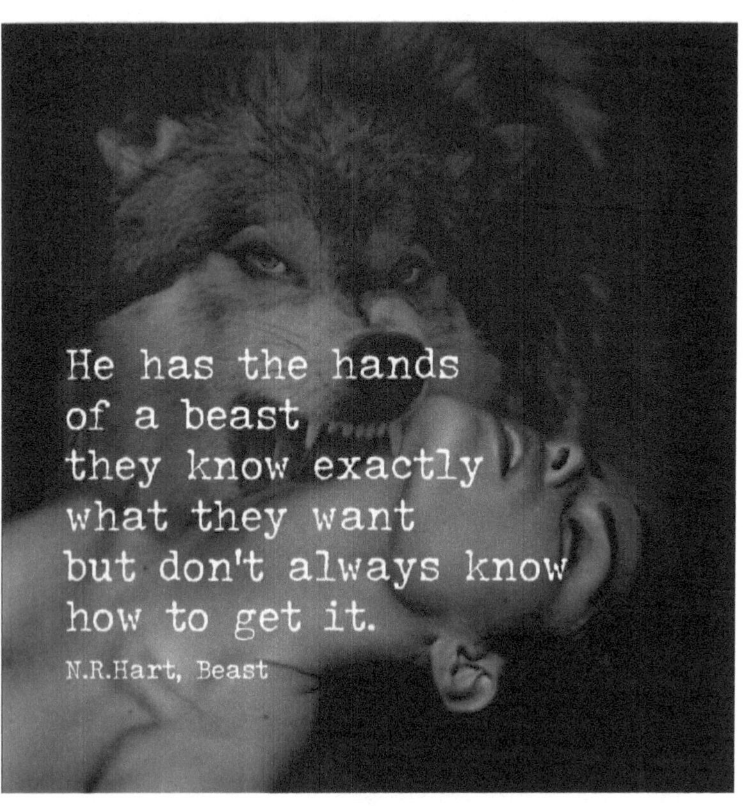
He has the hands
of a beast
they know exactly
what they want
but don't always know
how to get it.
N.R.Hart, Beast

Hellfire Kisses

You lost her and it wasn't
because
you didn't love her
instead, you were scared
of her love
scared of your feelings
for her...
of not being in control
of a love
that made you feel too much...
You can keep your ordinary
love
with your ordinary kisses.
I only want kisses from
hellfire
and a thunderous love
cracking my heart in two.
I only ever wanted you. -N.R.Hart

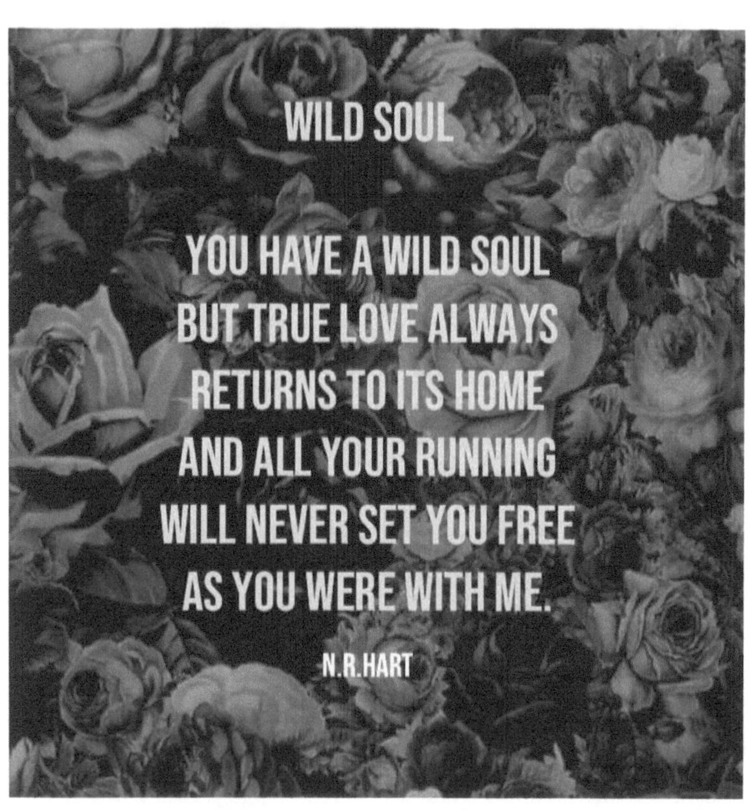

WILD SOUL

YOU HAVE A WILD SOUL
BUT TRUE LOVE ALWAYS
RETURNS TO ITS HOME
AND ALL YOUR RUNNING
WILL NEVER SET YOU FREE
AS YOU WERE WITH ME.

N.R.HART

I imagine a hot summer's night
you are driving and my hand
is inside yours and the heat
suddenly becomes unbearable.
You pull over reaching for me
our hands and mouths groping
each other
you open the door and pick me up
placing me on top of the hood
taking me right there
fast and hard
and the only sound I hear
is my body screaming your name.
-N.R.Hart

"in-between"

I existed somewhere
in-between
holding on and letting
go
afraid to lose the rest
of you
afraid to lose the rest
of me.
            -N.R.Hart

My eyes told you everything

They don't see you like I do
they know nothing of you
such a simple love
such a little love
they know nothing of the layers
the intricate layers
the complexities of the man
hiding underneath.
How the light never reaches
your eyes when you smile.
Our love was big. Our love was hard.
I sat with you in the darkness
and kissed away your sadness.
I looked into your eyes and saw
your soul.
My eyes told you everything.
Why weren't you listening?

-N.R.Hart

She always wanted it
to be him...
she longed to hear those
words he whispered
making her tremble again
and again.
The pictures he would paint
in her mind sending
shock waves of pleasure
through her.
She had a weakness
for him...
and ache for his touch
a longing for his kiss.
He was just something
she couldn't resist.

-N.R.Hart / "irresistible"

It was a mad passionate
love. A love like that
was unforgettable.
Hearts on fire
always remembering
never forgetting ...
you don't get over a love
like that...
it lives inside you burning
through everything.
Lost lovers hell bent
on finding their way back
again.   —N. R. Hart

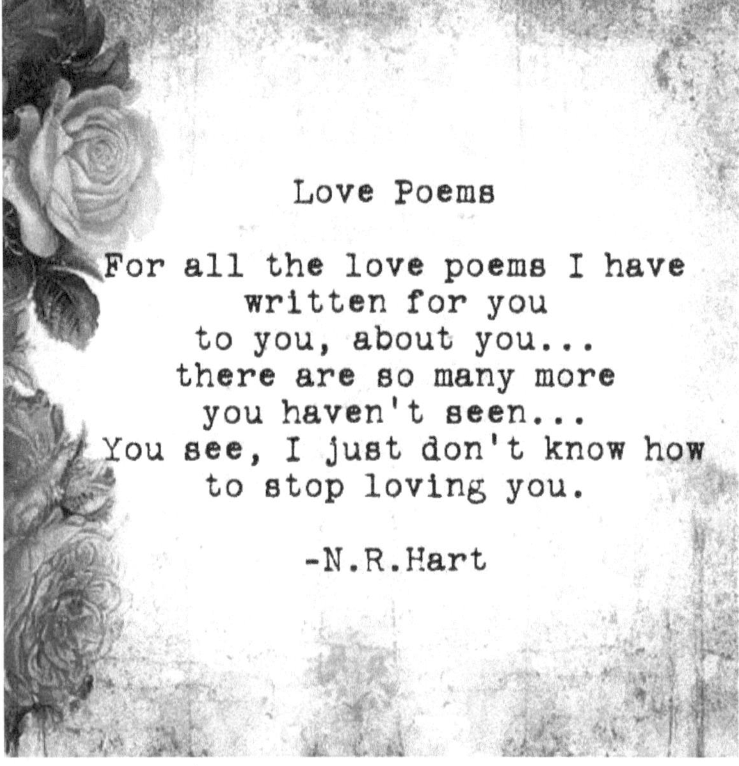

Love Poems

For all the love poems I have
written for you
to you, about you...
there are so many more
you haven't seen...
You see, I just don't know how
to stop loving you.

-N.R.Hart

They say opposites attract
but we were too much alike
from the start
you were something
I understood...
sometimes, all too well.
Because understanding you
meant loving you
way too much.

Even more than I should.

-N.R.Hart "loving you"

I would
rearrange
the stars
and align
the planets
hang the moon
and collide
like comets
cause madness
and mayhem
just to love you
again.

-N.R.Hart

She writes for them
even though
they may not hear her.
She writes because
she misses the sound
of yesterday.
She writes every day
for the unwavering burn.
She writes of him
forever...
until his return.

-N.R.Hart "return"

Magnificent Seas

Loving you was like falling into
the deepest parts of the ocean
my feet no longer firmly planted
on the ground
drifting alongside the treacherous
waves in your eyes
tangled up in your riptides.
There are no shallow depths with you
no safety net.
I only want to wander your magnificent
seas until I am drowning in you
and you are drowning in me.

-N.R.Hart

Maybe you weren't mine
but it felt like we
belonged to each other
and I loved you as though
you were mine.
                    -N.R.Hart

Moonlight Madness

There has always been
something unspoken
between us.
A magical pull
of the Universe
burning stars and
moonlight and madness
and midnight.
A divine force
that is out of our control.
Something unexplainable
I do to you.
Something unexplainable
you do to me.
                    -N.R.Hart

I remember sitting there with you
in the burning sunlight
staring into your eyes and wanting
nothing more than to escape inside them
softly melting into one another as the rest
of the world fell away...
and it was just the two of us sweetly soaking
in each other's presence.
You tenderly put your arm around me
kissing my forehead as you held my hair
in your hands
and we just sat there for the longest time
saying nothing.
And, I wondered how it was,
I could feel so peaceful with you and
at the same time, *on fire*.
                              -N.R.Hart *"on fire"*

And I am going to
kiss you
so that you feel it
deep down into
your bones
and the crevice
of your soul.
-N.R.Hart

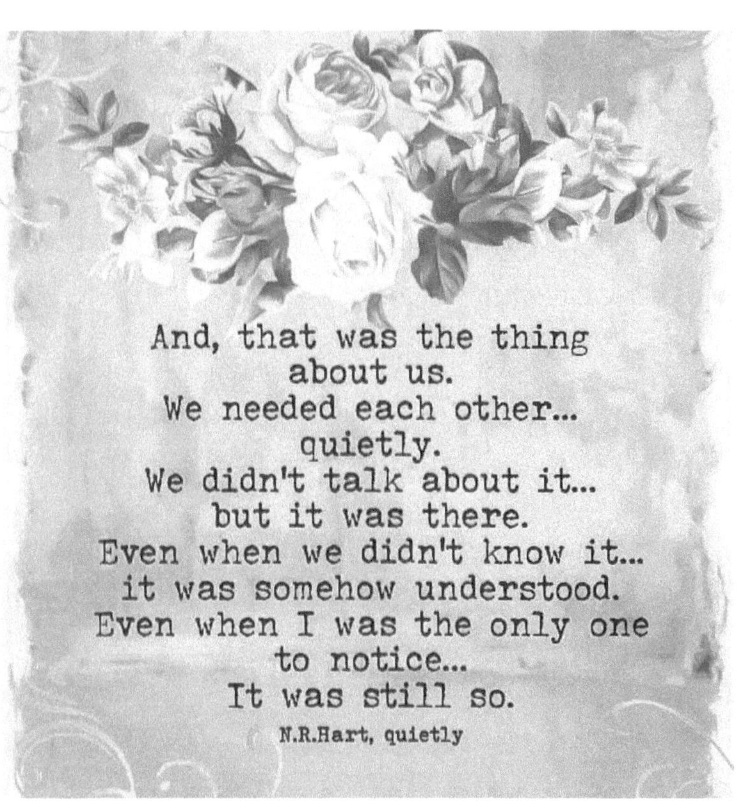

And, that was the thing
about us.
We needed each other...
quietly.
We didn't talk about it...
but it was there.
Even when we didn't know it...
it was somehow understood.
Even when I was the only one
to notice...
It was still so.
N.R.Hart, quietly

Twin Flames Dynamic

Two souls in love
one soul will stay
the other will go away
one soul will chase
the other will run
are they ever to merge
as one?
One soul is fire
the other is ice
one burns eternally
the other cold with regret
Two souls in love
living near and far
dying together and apart.

-N.R.Hart (Runner and Chaser)

116

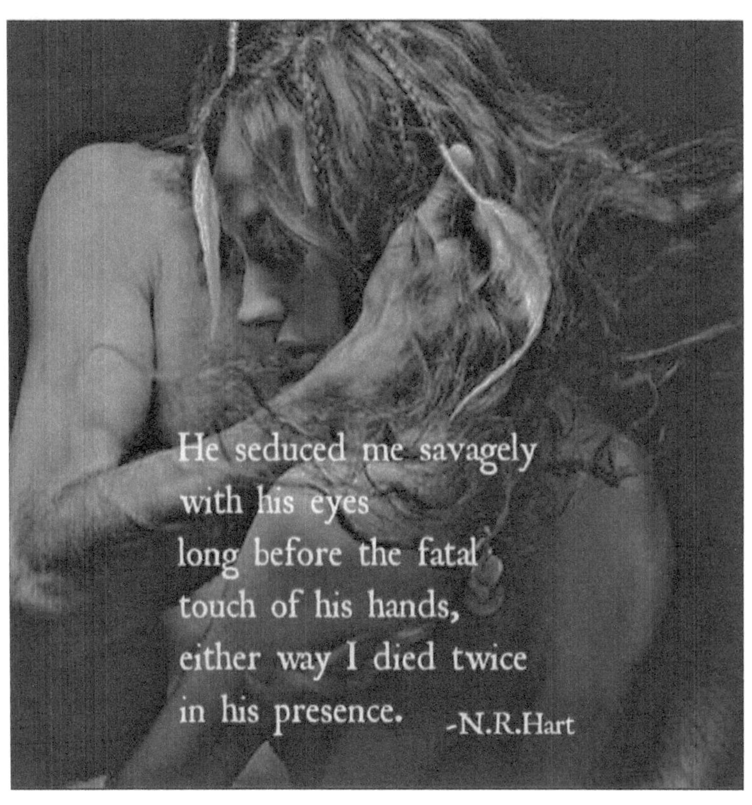

He seduced me savagely
with his eyes
long before the fatal
touch of his hands,
either way I died twice
in his presence.   -N.R.Hart

He made me love him
for the way I felt alive
with him.
He awoke in me a secret
midnight
who now prefers the bite
of a wolf
hot blooded and true
chasing love and moonlight.

-N.R.Hart

"Secret midnight"

I love you because my soul never forgets (part III)

Once you have felt someone's soul
so much like your own
once you have satiated a hunger
your body has never known
once you have felt something
in your heart
you have never felt before
you can never go back to ordinary.
It will never be enough.
I will never feel again
the way I felt for you.
There is only one soul love.
Just one. Just you.
It will die, only when I do.

-N.R.Hart , soul love

Soul Lovers

It wasn't like we could control it
it was always there between us
this deep connection
this strong physical attraction
this intense chemistry.
A powerful emotional bond
connected by an invisible red string
and though this string had been
pulled to its breaking point
it never breaks, it never does.
This twin energy of the universe
keeps us spiritually and soulfully
connected. Unable to control it,
it controls us instead.
We were soul lovers.
We were the lovers our bodies
always remember.
We were the lovers our souls
never forget.

N.R.Hart,   Soul Lovers

Spellbound

We have our own little world
you and I...
and how everything stops
including time.
I feel your words touching me
whispering things
demanding things
your sweet deadly words.
I fall apart. I fall for you.
And, I am under your spell
again.
My only desire is for you
to possess me
to dominate me. Make me yours.
Feel me come undone
in your hands...
how I surrender to you.
My mind my body my soul.
Love me. Take me. All of me.

-N.R.Hart   "Spellbound" ©

Star-crossed lovers part2

Are we just star-crossed
lovers
revolving around each other
like drifting galaxies
shooting stars
reaching and missing
hoping and wishing
on one another...
aching to love in every
Universe
living for the day
our worlds finally collide.

-N.R.Hart

The most dangerous love
is the kind that starts a fire
in you that will not die and
every part of you is awakened...
from then on every other love
pales in comparison
never coming close to that alive
feeling you once had...
and what scares you the most is
what if you never love like that again?
As you feel yourself slowly dying
inside that cruelest realization.
-N.R.Hart

"Twin Flames" (a paradox)

Meeting your twin flame will be one of the strongest, most powerful connections in your life. And, it may also be the most confusing and difficult ones too. There is only one twin flame and not everyone has met theirs in their lifetime.
But, you will know immediately once you come across them, the connection is so pure and fiery, they will feel strangely familiar to you. It will almost be an out-of-control feeling.
One that scares you and excites you at the same time.
You are left breathless...and yet, there is a stillness inside of you. There will be complete chaos...and yet, you will feel at peace.
Almost as if you cannot be apart, but you cannot be together, either. You cannot live with them but you cannot live without them.
You feel as though nothing can replace the emptiness they leave behind and they sense this same emptiness...and they are on their way back to you...every time.
Even though the world keeps trying to pull apart what the universe knows should be together.
They can reunite many times in a lifetime.
Twin Flames can be the biggest paradox because they are literally the other half of your soul in another person...fighting to exist apart....And, simply cannot. -N.R.Hart

Their chemistry was volatile from
the start..friends, lovers, soulmates
they were all of it together.
They were connected by a fiery energy
on a deep soulful level with an intense
magnetic attraction to one another.
Not only were their minds in sync
reading one another's thoughts, so
were their bodies.
He knew her body like the back of his
hand. He knew when she needed a soft
caress or a firm grip. How she craved
the fine line between pleasure and
pain. He knew what she needed even
before she knew herself. He knew how to
give her what she was afraid to ask for.

And, just like twin flames that will not
die, it lives inside you burning
you alive.   —N.R.Hart (twin flames)

Unbreakable

When they ask me about you
I could never really explain
it...explain us.
How even after all the love
and the madness
the joy and the heartbreak
I still could not let go of you.
What they did not understand
was the bond between us
that was created long ago.
We were an ancient love
older than any love story
ever told.
Where it remains invincible.
It goes well beyond the physical realm
and resides somewhere deep
in the soul dimension.
We were fragile, you and I,
so very fragile.
And yet, we were unbreakable. -N.R.Hart

I don't know how else
to explain it other than
we work, we just work
the two of us....
and it's natural
and insanely hot
and completely mind-blowing
all at once.
The sweet bliss in the knowing
we just "get" one another
the utter comfort of being
in the presence of
a soulmate.
Because, it was just understood
between the two of us...
that I was your favorite person
and you were mine.

-N.R.Hart "understood"©

"Unfathomable" Twin Flame
I sat there for the longest time
frozen in silence knowing in my heart
there will never be another like you.
Like us. We are something like
unfathomable together...
we don't make sense but actually when we
are together we make more sense than
anything else. It's like nothing
I have ever felt with anyone.   n.r.hart©
I remember every last detail about us.
You are a twin flame...a part of who I am.
And now sitting here next to you
I cannot say these words to you
because sometimes pulling them out
from the darkest crevice of your soul
where fear resides...fear of losing hope.
There is so much hope with you.
For more time together. More unfathomable
moments with you...
And there is so much to remember.
How can we forget when we gave each other
so much to remember...   - N.R. Hart

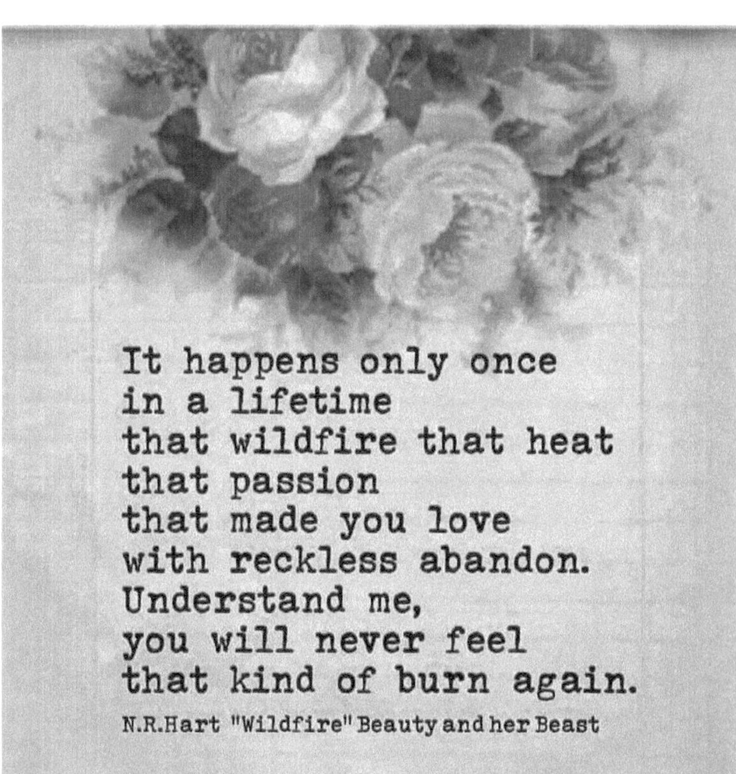

It happens only once
in a lifetime
that wildfire that heat
that passion
that made you love
with reckless abandon.
Understand me,
you will never feel
that kind of burn again.
N.R.Hart "Wildfire" Beauty and her Beast

wildflower soul

Lean in hard
your wildflower soul
next to mine
let us bend and crash
and break
let us kiss and fall
and be.
Let us heal and laugh
and love.
Let us be us.
Let us begin again.

N.R.Hart , begin again

Your Name

I knew you were different
the moment I laid eyes
on you...
something about you was always
too much.
You made me feel everything
so intensely
every feeling I felt all
at once...
all these feelings living
inside me
making them yours
all of them with your name.

-N.R.Hart

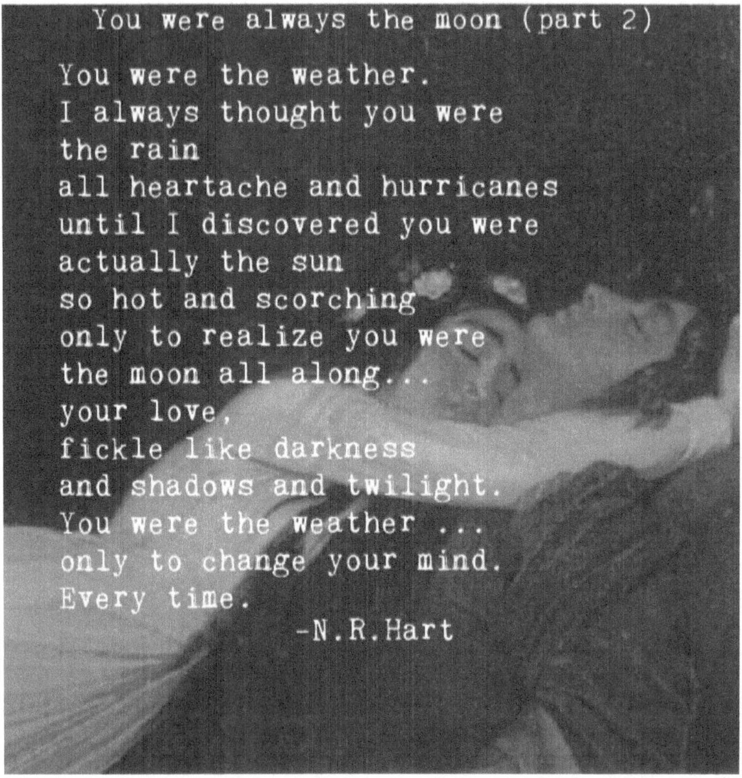

      You were always the moon (part 2)

You were the weather.
I always thought you were
the rain
all heartache and hurricanes
until I discovered you were
actually the sun
so hot and scorching
only to realize you were
the moon all along...
your love,
fickle like darkness
and shadows and twilight.
You were the weather ...
only to change your mind.
Every time.
                    -N.R.Hart

Passion!

I want a passion so hot that being
with that one person is all you can
think about and no one else will do.
A passion that consumes you
the kind you lose sleep over
tossing and turning with a feverish
desire and your only thought is when
will you be with them again?
The anticipation of it all
the build-up of it all
the longing, the waiting, the burning
the hair pulling, the melting of bodies
the desperation of hungry mouths
ready to devour
the groping of hands, the tearing off
of clothes
the primal ache of a lover's touch
of wanting more and more
an insatiable hunger that is never
satisfied
I want a passion that makes me feel
wildly alive...or nothing at all. -N.R.Hart

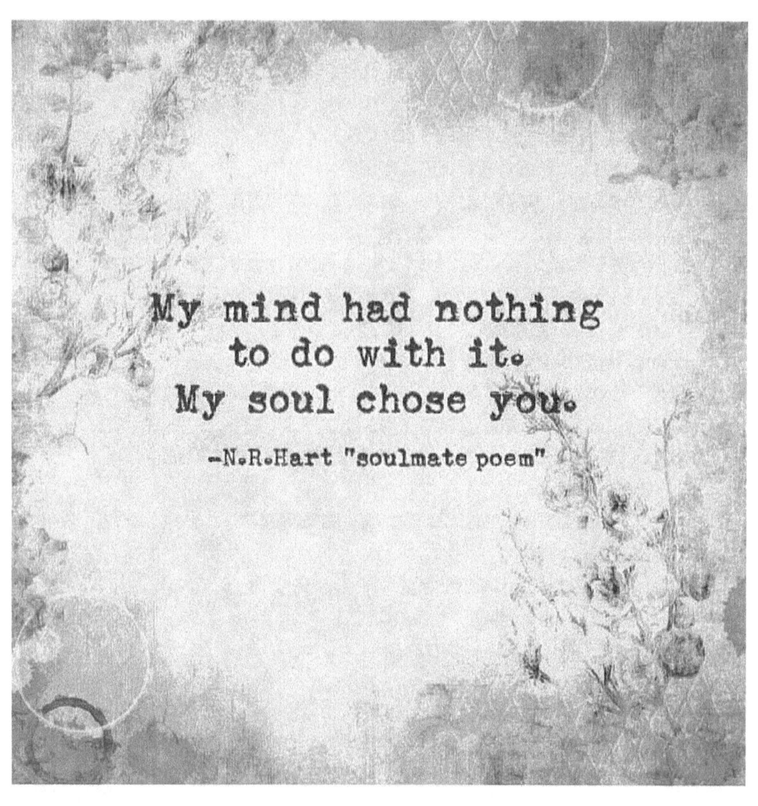

My mind had nothing
to do with it.
My soul chose you.

-N.R.Hart "soulmate poem"

An Autumn Season

"My soul and your soul
are forever tangled." ©

N.R.Hart

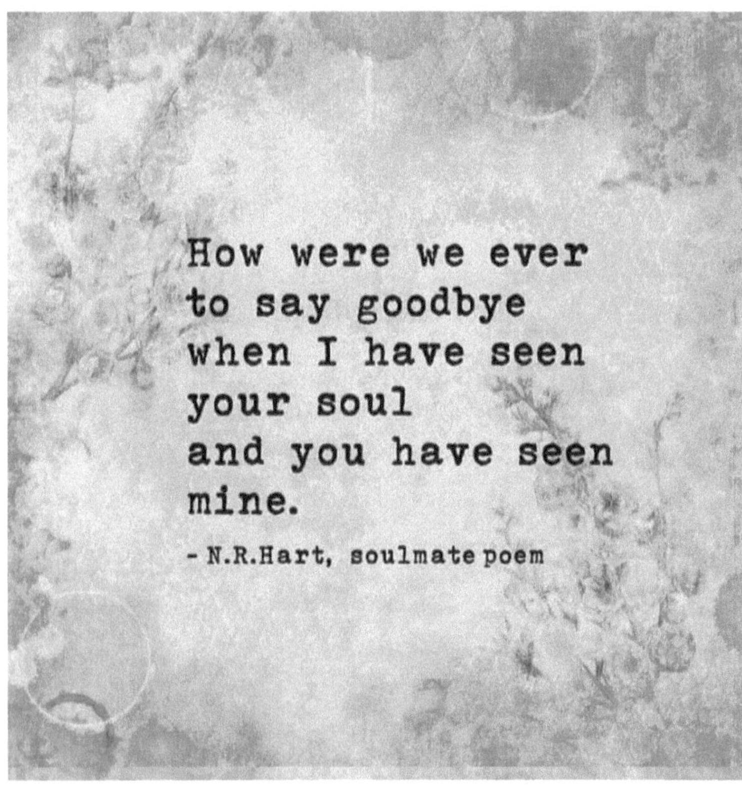

How were we ever
to say goodbye
when I have seen
your soul
and you have seen
mine.

- N.R.Hart, soulmate poem

I wonder where you are tonight
  as I sit here   all alone
I tried so many ways to tell you
yet my secret is still unknown
you're so far away but oh,
how I wanted you to know
how long I have waited to love you
and tell you so.
-N.R.Hart

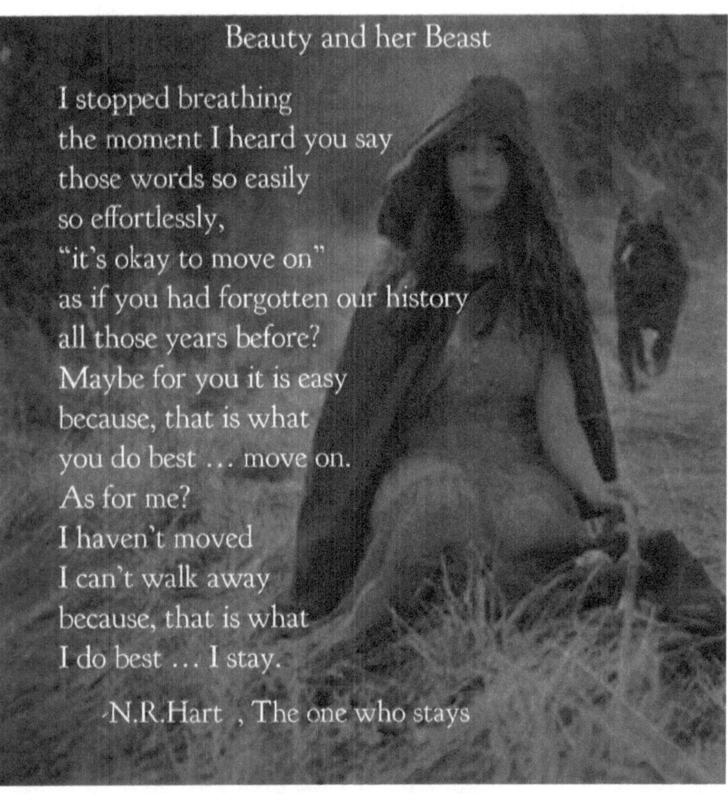

Beauty and her Beast

I stopped breathing
the moment I heard you say
those words so easily
so effortlessly,
"it's okay to move on"
as if you had forgotten our history
all those years before?
Maybe for you it is easy
because, that is what
you do best ... move on.
As for me?
I haven't moved
I can't walk away
because, that is what
I do best ... I stay.

-N.R.Hart , The one who stays

If you are alone
and I will sit there with you
if you are weak
and I will give you my blood
my bones
if you are scared
and I will hold you close
and closer still
if you can no longer live
and I will love you
back to life.
I feel so much of you
inside me
and I am no longer certain
where you begin and I end.

-N.R.Hart "beginning and end"

This thing we have
goes beyond reason
it's our souls
fighting
for each other
even when our eyes
couldn't see.

-N.R.Hart

A True Lover

A true lover is the one
who knows all your secret desires
and gives them to you
without you having to ask
they understand how your body
responds
they are in harmony
with your mind
and one with your soul.

- N.R.Hart

Wildest dreams

One look one touch
one kiss...
this desire becomes fire
this love becomes life
my body melts into yours
a complete surrendering
of souls...
You make my fantasies
come alive.
My wildest dreams come
true.

-N.R.Hart "wildest dreams"©

your touch

Your touch alone
holds the power
to save and
destroy me
all at once...
and I am dying
for either.

-N.R.Hart

Do you think you have
a choice in loving someone?
The answer will always be...no.
Your soul picks who you love
and your heart seals the deal.
How little a choice we have
over such things when
your heart knows what it wants
and your soul knows when it's real.

N.R. Hart

"heart and soul"

Whether fate stepped in
she only knew
one thing;
she was supposed
to be with him
a lover a friend
a secret or a sin.

-N.R.Hart

Moonlight Lovers

Loving you was my escape
into sweet oblivion
our souls free in each other
the loving came easy
kissing on carhoods
driving into neon nights
passion igniting
in-between stoplights.
Any destination...
is where our love landed.
The earth moved for us
in a blazing trail of fire
lighting up our universe
only moonlight lovers see
it fell from the sky
onto you and me.

-N.R.Hart

"Heartbreak"

It's okay if you fall down
again and again...
thinking you were over it.
Life is messy. So is love...
You may have to pick
yourself back up
many times...
if the pain is deep.
You cannot hurry the
healing.
In some ways you may never
get over it.
It takes as long as it takes.
Maybe even a lifetime...

-N.R.Hart

History

You can come up with
every excuse in the book
try and talk yourself
into believing it...
none of that matters
because with some people
it will never be over...

-N.R.Hart

History

They say you can never compete
with history and I say they
are right. There is too much to
compete with.
You can never compete with the
greatest of loves.
Too much time spent. Too many years
together.
Too much familiarity. Too many
memories...
Too much to remember.
Too much to forget.
Too much love felt...
Too many kisses shared.
You can never compare the
"good old days" to the new.
This is why every love song
every poem...is about us.
About you.   -N.R.Hart

A love that only
gets stronger
with time
and I whisper
quietly
be still, my heart.
N.R.Hart, be still my heart

150

It's the connection to
someone the friendship...
that makes you feel
comforted.
True love is born from true
intimacy.
Because losing a lover is
bad
but losing your best friend
is worse.

-N.R.Hart "Intimacy"

Our love story is what legends
are made from
a pure friendship a real romance
the best of both worlds
laughter and kisses
the fervor of passion
with bite marks and bruised lips
holding hands and fingerprints
pressed against flesh
the thrill of being alive
our souls stained with eternity
and sweet poetry.
A love like nothing you have
experienced before or ever will
again. Except with me. -N.R.Hart

And, if for some reason
I do finally give up on you
just know it took everything
I had and I mean everything
inside me....
how it crushed my heart
killed my soul
I have never fought for anything
the way I fought for you.
I lived and breathed you
and used every last breath
to keep you here with me.
I have died more than once
for you...
and I don't know how many
little deaths I have left in me.
    -N.R.Hart "little deaths"

There are some moments
so special so everlasting
that words aren't even
necessary
like when I saw you again
after a long time
of missing you...
This was one of those times.

-N.R.Hart

She was never hard
to love but,
forgetting her will be.

N.R.Hart

I stopped breathing the moment
you opened your mouth
for I never knew what words
would slip out...
It can be something as breathtaking
as let's go for a drive or as devastating
as I am leaving.
I am always prepared for the worst
to come pouring out of your mouth
the one I can't stop staring at
the one I crave kissing constantly
and yet it is the same one
enveloping me in terror...
gripping whatever I can reach for
as I suffocate in my own darkness
for I have become used to my world
crumbling around you.   -N.R.Hart

Once upon a time you were mine.

N.R.HART

Say you will be mine...
we are running out of time.

If you were to ask me
what I don't want to be
without in this life, maybe
it would be this...
feeling your eyes on me
penetrating me...
especially when I look away
the feel of your hands anywhere
and everywhere...
your strength against my softness
my weakness for your touch...
just being in your presence
how you calm me
and set me on fire
all at once...
I can be without most things
in this life...
but one of them isn't you.

-N.R.Hart, The Last of the Romantics

Love Story

So many love stories
happen and remain untold
they just disappear...
I wrote our love story
so we would remember it
so we wouldn't just disappear.
We are the lucky ones.

-N.R.Hart   Love story

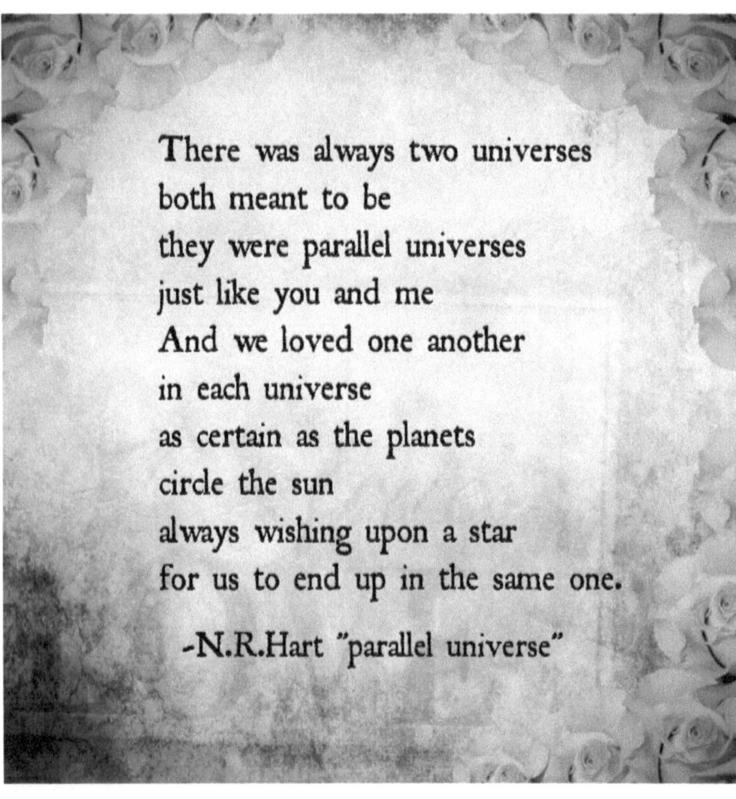

There was always two universes
both meant to be
they were parallel universes
just like you and me
And we loved one another
in each universe
as certain as the planets
circle the sun
always wishing upon a star
for us to end up in the same one.

-N.R.Hart "parallel universe"

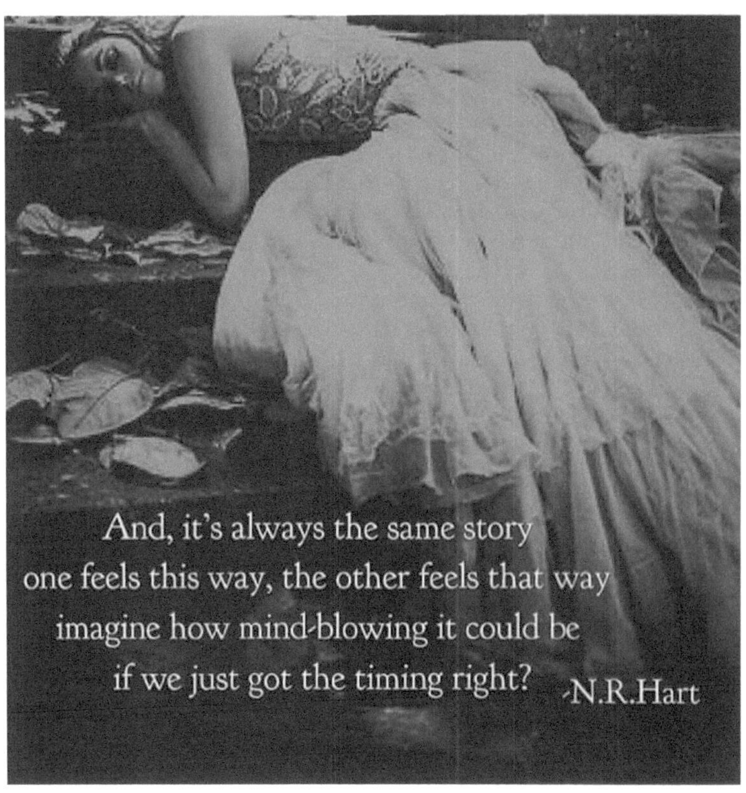

And, it's always the same story
one feels this way, the other feels that way
imagine how mind-blowing it could be
if we just got the timing right?   -N.R.Hart

Phoenix

She looked up to him
her twin flame
the light in her heart
the fire in her soul
he shone brighter than all the rest.
Until one day his light was gone
leaving her in the dark.
And, in the depths of her own despair
she rose higher and burned brighter
than ever before,
leaving him in the dust.
And, to this day
he still aches for her passion
he still yearns for her flame
and maybe in the end
this was her revenge.

-N.R.Hart

Haunted

She felt his eyes
on her
always watching
over her
and then she knew
being haunted was
for the living too.

-N.R.Hart

Queen of Hearts ♥

They call me the
Queen of Hearts
I will always fight for you
I will always fight for love
because I will fight
for the rest of my life.

-N.R.Hart "Queen of Hearts" ©

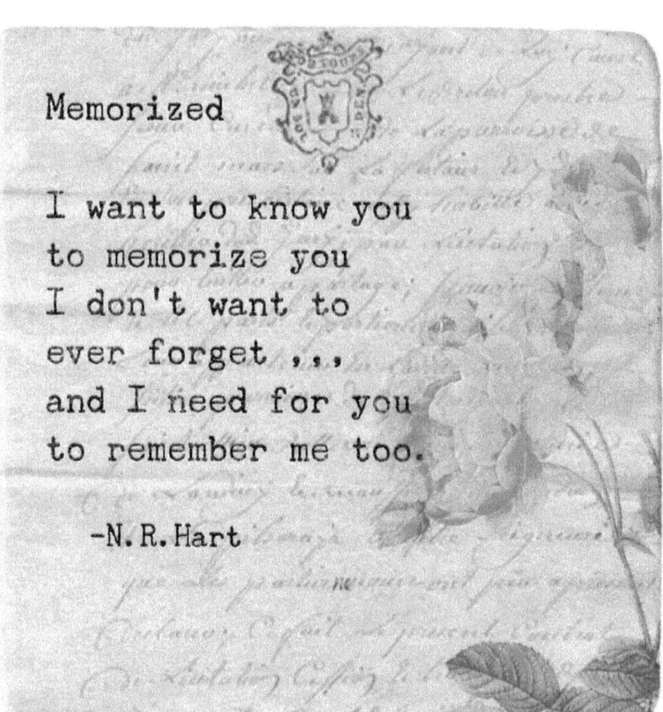

Memorized

I want to know you
to memorize you
I don't want to
ever forget ...
and I need for you
to remember me too.

-N.R.Hart

You and I...
We were so similar
We shared the same
mind
The same spirit
The same soul
It was like coming home.
N.R.Hart "Beauty and her Beast"

166

"Screaming hearts"

How long do we go on pretending like
neither one of us exists?
That what we shared was nothing short
of e*pic.*
How much silence do we put between us
(all the while our hearts screaming)
to prove we are no longer in love?
All the miles and the distance
will never silence *this love.*
How many times have you tried in vain to replace
what we had only to discover that we were
once in a lifetime?
What if we got it all wrong?
What if we spend our entire lives , both of us needing
each other this whole time, *and never knowing it?*

-N.R.Hart

Seasons of the Heart (part II)

You are nowhere and everywhere...
I remember how we spent those
summers beneath the trees
the gentle breeze gives me goosebumps
I can still feel you here...
and I recall how much greener the grass
was with your smile
how much warmer the sun was with your mouth
how much bluer the sky was with your eyes
how much wilder the wind was with your hands
how much sweeter this world was with you in it.
How we took it all by storm and turned it
upside down.
Remember when this was our town?
How a brilliant romance happened here...
every day we spent was a miracle we never
understood , until now.
And, when you go back to our town
you be sure to tell them ..."it was the time
of our lives." just like I would.
Now we are reminded of everything we lack,
would we have walked away if we knew
we couldn't go back?

-N.R.Hart , "our town"

"Seasons of the Heart"

I have such a hard time believing
we went through all that
all those years together...
all the friendship
the flirting, the teasing
the fighting, the making up
the passion...
the persistence of love
and love and love...
through every summer,
every spring, every fall,
every winter.
I have loved you through
every season...
just to lose it all
in the end.

-N.R.Hart, "Seasons of the Heart"

"Souls on Fire"

Deep down, even though we never said it
we both knew what we meant to each other.
We both knew. To talk about it felt, *small.*
Together, we were *larger than life.*
And I wonder, how did you lose sight of yourself
and everything you held so dear?
That burning desire to dig deeper for all those things that
set your soul on fire. So afraid to be yourself, you have
given in to mediocrity and playing it safe.
How can you show your true-self to me yet *truly* love another?
This is why you run but, you can never hide
from the beast that lurks inside.
And, this is why you are scared of us. Scared of our passion.
Our fire. How real we are together.
This is why you settle for something lesser than us.
Something easier than us. *Anything to escape your own soul.*
But I promise you, you will always hunger for something more.
You are capable of so much more than what you've settled for.

   -N.R.Hart "be with someone who sets your soul on fire."

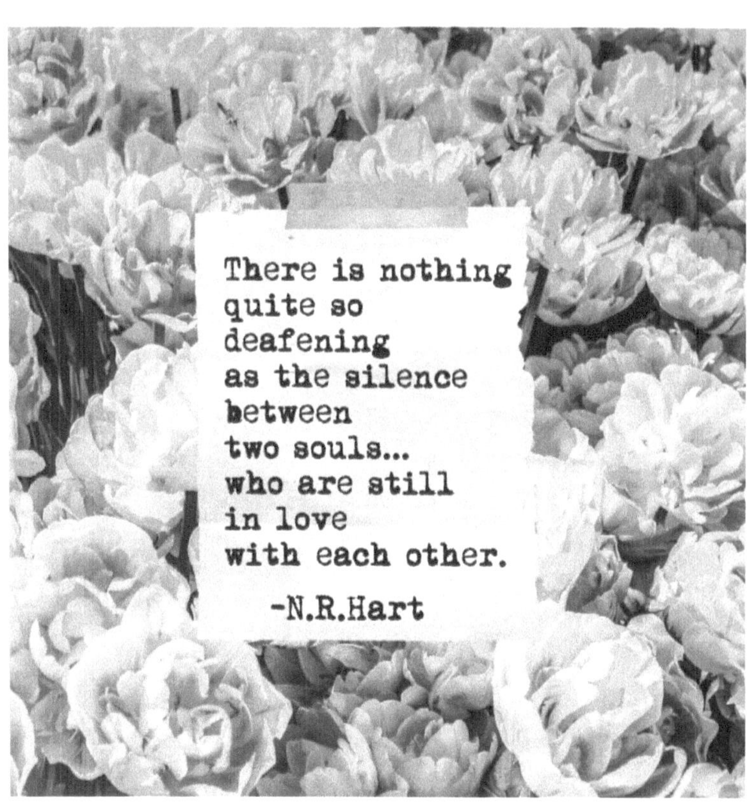

There is nothing
quite so
deafening
as the silence
between
two souls...
who are still
in love
with each other.

-N.R.Hart

"Soulmates are forever"

Some loves are deeper
some loves are grander
than the rest.
There will never be closure,
you foolish thing.
How this love haunts you...
its sharp edges carved into
your bones
memories you carry around
like a home.
How many poems must a poet pen,
how many ways to be clever?
To prove that soulmates are
forever.
                -N.R.Hart

And, remember...
the greatest love
stories
are always the hardest
love stories
they persist and persist
and you keep fighting
for them
again and again...
This is how you know
they are great.

N.R.Hart "The Greatest Love Stories"

This is the story I never knew how to write and this
poetry is the unspoken words of my life.
The day you walked into that coffee shop standing there
looking at me...I knew you were different the moment I laid
eyes on you because I thought this one...holds the power to
love me in ways that can break me. I knew that encounter was
no accident and was always meant to be. It was as if you blew
in like a storm cloud from the sky up above, suddenly and
without warning...changing our lives in ways I have yet to
discover. Our souls recognized each other long before we
ever knew and so began our own language of love. We never
had to say much, in fact words seemed to get in the way. We
were better without them. We had a quiet understanding
between souls instead. And, this is by far more powerful
than any language spoken. Our eyes said everything...
every unspoken word could be understood with just a look.
Our hearts knew what was to be and eventually we found our
way. I believe it was inevitable for us to love one another
in many shapes and forms throughout time. The passion
between us was our souls catching fire and this kind of
love is a once in a lifetime love. And, no matter what
happens between you...it will never die.
So on that day you blew into my life like a storm cloud and
wrapped yourself around my heart...it was a storm we could
no longer outrun. The only relief was to stand still
and let it pour. -N.R.Hart " storm cloud"

"The problem with love"

The problem with love is...
Love is not supposed to be hard.
Love can be the easiest thing
in the world.
To feel. To show. To know. To do.
But, we make it hard.
And, because of this love itself
becomes hard.
Love now becomes confusing
and scary and complicated.
And, this is why we have so much
trouble holding onto love.
Because we want so badly to love but,
we get in our own way.
And, this is why love becomes
uncertain...unfinished...unforgettable.

-N.R.Hart

I always thought
I was the beauty
saving you
as it turns out
you were my beast
and saved me right back.

-N.R.Hart "Beauty and her Beast"

Twin Flame (Journey)

You may think the twin flame journey is a peaceful one, being reunited
with your twin flame. Understand that there is a state of euphoria,
a sense of relief and happiness that overwhelms you, finally
being in their presence. Time stops when you are together
and nothing else exists except the two of you.
It just feels right to be with one another.
But, at the same time you can be consumed with feelings of confusion
and fear and denial throughout the journey.
It can be a dangerous love. Many are scared and don't know what
to do with the intensity of their feelings where you can experience
a passion and desire that is out of control.
It can be an impossible love. One that makes you feel too much
all at once. Some run from it or deny that the feelings even exist.
It is almost as if you cannot live with them but you cannot live
without them either.
Many twin flames can be separated more times throughout
their lives than they are together.
And, this separation is a different kind of agony...going against
your soul like that. It will cause you a lifetime of unrest.
Your eyes always searching for them. -N.R.Hart

Twin Flames
My heart loves you
my body craves you
but it's my soul
that needs to be
next to yours.

-M.R.Hart

The most romantic
thing in the world
is feeling
understood.

-N.R.Hart

Our love didn't have to
make sense.
Our souls understood
one another
and that's all that mattered.

-N.R.Hart "soulmate poem" ©2018

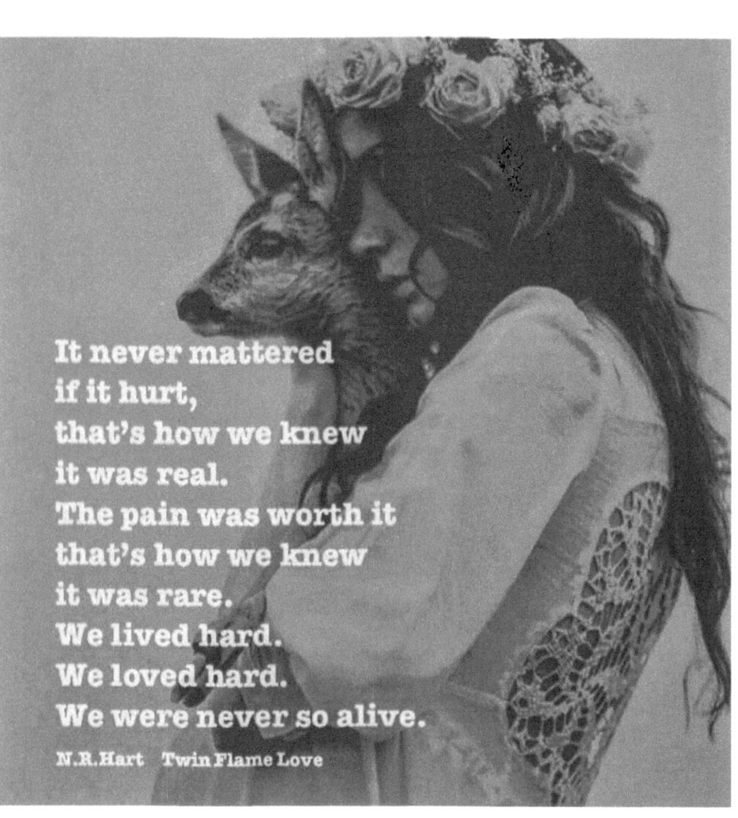

It never mattered
if it hurt,
that's how we knew
it was real.
The pain was worth it
that's how we knew
it was rare.
We lived hard.
We loved hard.
We were never so alive.
N.R.Hart   Twin Flame Love

ONE DAY YOU WILL COME ACROSS SOMEONE
WHOSE SOUL FEELS TOO FAMILIAR TO YOURS.
THEY WILL SHARE THE SAME PASSIONS
QUIRKS AND INTERESTS
THEY ARE THE MIRROR IMAGE OF US.
THEY WILL UNDERSTAND YOU IN A WAY
NO ONE EVER HAS OR WILL.
THIS PERSON WILL TURN OUT TO BE
THE LOVE OF YOUR LIFE.
THIS PERSON WILL TURN OUT TO BE
YOUR TWIN FLAME.
YOU SHARE MORE IN COMMON WITH THEM THAN
ANYONE.
BUT, THE MOST UNIMAGINABLE TRUTH...
YOU MAY NOT SHARE YOUR LIVES TOGETHER.

N.R.HART, TWIN FLAME TRUTH

Twin Flame

No matter where I go
my eyes will never stop
searching for you...
I am looking for the
other half of my soul.

-N.R.Hart

ABOUT THE AUTHOR

N.R.Hart started writing poetry at a young age and used her poetry as a way to express her innermost thoughts and emotions. A true romantic at heart, she expresses feelings of love, hope, passion, despair, vulnerability and romance in her poetry. Trapping time forever and a keeper of memories is what she loves most about the enduring power of poetry. Her poetry has been so eloquently described as "words delicately placed inside a storm." Poetry is here to make us feel instead of think; as thinking is for the mind and poetry is for the heart and soul. N.R.Hart hopes to open up your heart and touch your soul with her poetry.

"Poetry is not dead, it is alive
in the minds of those
who feel...instead of think." ©

N.R.Hart

Connect with N.R.Hart:
Facebook@N.R.Hart, Author
Facebook@PearlsSlippingOffAString
Instagram@N.R.Hart
Twitter@nrhartpoetry